A Recipe for Restaurant Success

Charles Okwalinga

Dedication

I dedicate this book to my late father, Reuben Ojulo, who worked the land and instilled upon me that diligent hard work leads to success. I also thank my Mother, and my step Mother, who worked hard with my father to forge an education for me in the early years, practicing 'illiterate economics', enterprise without formal education, while managing a business that sustained us as a family.

Acknowledgments

I acknowledge and thank my wife, Margaret Okwalinga, for demonstrating my first glimpses of professional and creative cooking. Margaret and I have worked diligently over the years, from the initial concept of fine dining African cuisine, which eventually led to our involvement in the industry and running an excellent food establishment. Margaret and I built our business from scratch with modest means and a young family. In many ways, we demonstrated that it is possible. I also need to acknowledge and thank my children for their support, withstanding the times without us at home due to long shifts, and sacrificing themselves to ensure we remained financially secure even when there was no other place to turn to.

I would also like to acknowledge the staff of Exceline Restaurant. Their dedication to our business has enabled us to create and sustain excellent and professional systems that has kept the business going over the years.

Lastly, and very importantly, I would like to acknowledge Geoffrey Semaganda, (Action Wealth Group) for mentoring, consultanting, project managering and believing in me, working against all odds and challenges, to produce this book. Without him, my story would have remained in my head instead of helping others.

Whether fast food, formal dining, steak house, pizza parlour or coffee shop, start your journey here with this comprehensive guide to opening your own food establishment.

Table of Contents

SECTION 1: GETTING STARTED 11
    So Whose Idea Is It Anyway? 11
    So you want to open a restaurant 12
    History of Restaurants 12
    What makes a Successful Restaurateur 14
    Today's Restaurant Trends 17
    Research, Research, Research 20
    Building Your Business Plan 23
    First Financials 32
    Finding Funding (Investors) 34

SECTION 2: CORRECTLY FORMULATING A FOOD SERVICE CONCEPT 37
    The Types and Styles of Restaurants 37
    Formality 46
    Quick Service versus Sit Down Service 47

Take away or Deliver to them 48

Alcohol / Bar service 48

Studying Competition 49

Ambiance and Architecture 50

Identifying Functions of the Restaurant Space,
Fine Dining or Partying 51

Marketing and Branding 52

Section 3: Property / Premises:
To Buy or To Lease 53

Location, Location, Location 53

The Benefits of Buying a Property 54

The Benefits of Leasing Property 55

Parking, entrance, frontage, kitchen, bar location, facilities 56

Creative Arrangements 56

Section 4: The Basics of Running a Restaurant ... 57

Working the Business Plan 57

Setting up the operations 58

Dealing with suppliers and procurement 59

Management and Production 62

Keeping the audits/ reviews of day running 63

Money matters, Takings 64

Identifying Fixed Costs and Variable Costs 65

Contracts 66

    Food Safety 67

    How to Create Schedules, Rotas 72

    Kitchen Schedules 74

    Front Office (Floor) and Upper Office (Admin) Schedules 75

    Staying Organised 76

    How to Manage a Restaurant Worker 78

    Compliance matters 79

    Music, Entertainment 80

SECTION 5: BUILDING THE BEST STAFF 83

    The Key Positions of Restaurant Staff 83

    Building a Better Front of House Staff 86

    Building a Better Kitchen Staff 87

    How to Hire Staff 89

    Employee Introduction and Training 91

    Health and Safety at Work 94

    Providing Customer Service 96

    Employee Manual 97

SECTION 6: COMPOSING THE MENU AND FOOD SERVICE DELIVERY 99

    The Basics of Menu Science 99

    Starters and Bites 102

    The Main Menu 103

    Portion Control 104

Table offering and presentation 106

Desserts 107

Money sense of the Menu 108

Bar and Beverage 109

How to Price the Food and Booze 110

Cross Selling and Upselling on menus 112

SECTION 7: THE PRE-OPENING 113

Deco and refurbishments 114

Buying Essential Equipment 117

Permits and Licenses 118

Point of Sales System (POS) 121

Credit Card Processing 123

Smallwares 124

Glassware, Dishes and Silverware 125

Initial stocking 127

Calling in the Compliance Inspectors 129

Putting Together an Opening Team 129

Choosing an Opening Date 130

Social Media Integration 131

Public Relations 132

SECTION 8: THE OPENING 135

The Friends/Family Test Run 136

Marketing Your Opening 137

Soft Opening/Grand Opening 138

Opening Day 139
Week One 142
Month One 144
Month Three 146
How to Remain 'New' Beyond the Opening 147

SECTION 9: THE NUMBERS OF RESTAURANT SUCCESS 149
Calculating Food Cost 150
Controlling Labour Cost 153
Hitting Your Expected Profit Margin 154
How to Price Your Menu Items 156

SECTION 10: HOW TO BUILD A LOYAL CLIENTELE 159
Quality 160
Giving your Audience the VIP Treatment 162
Loyalty Cards 164
Social Media Discounts 166
Going off the menu 167
Special Events and Promotions 169
Forging Long Term Relationships 171

SECTION 11: KEEPING YOUR RESTAURANT MODEL MODERN CURRENT AND RELEVANT 175
Understanding Trends 177
Knowing when and what to change. 179
New competitors 181
Staff Development 182

Time to expand services, develop additional segments 184
The Future of the Social Media Restaurant 186
Listening to feedback and reviews 186
Associations and Industry Collaborations 188

SECTION 12: TIPS TO LONG TERM SUCCESS 191
Time to Expand? 192
Closed for Renovations 193
When to Change Models 195
All Change, EXIT Strategy 197
All said (Write a Book) 199

ABOUT THE AUTHOR 201

Section [1]
Getting Started

SO WHOSE IDEA IS IT ANYWAY?

Many people want to open a restaurant. Sometimes, a family will make a large amount of money from another business, and decide to open their own restaurant. Other times, the person who wants to open a restaurant has a background in a completely different field. Sometimes, it might be someone with a background in finance or real estate, or it could be someone who has worked as a labourer. Many people who work in a restaurant spend their entire lives working towards opening their own restaurant. No matter what the circumstances, this book is meant to help people from all backgrounds when it comes to opening a restaurant. No matter who had the initial idea, you will find this book very helpful when it comes to navigating the complexities of opening a restaurant.

So you want to open a restaurant

Opening a restaurant can be a wonderful and challenging experience. For some, opening a restaurant is a dream come true. For others, it represents a new business venture. However you arrived at the decision to open a restaurant, having sound advice when it comes to running a restaurant operation is the main key to success.

Running a restaurant is very different than running a business in another industry. The profit margins are different, the type of employees vary, and you are sure to spend many holidays working while others are having fun with friends and family. This book was written to assist you from the concept formulation to the opening process. Within this book, you will learn how to calculate the financial workings of a restaurant operation, marketing strategies, buying equipment, menu design, to name but a few tasks you are sure to encounter during the opening.

To make this book accessible to the largest possible audience, the sections within this book have been written with the amateur in mind. At the same time, this book has been written to give experienced foodies a comprehensive outline of the opening process. No matter what your level of food or business experience, you are sure to benefit from the content written within this book.

History of Restaurants

The concept of the restaurant is a relatively new endeavour. While public eateries existed in Rome and early China, the concept we know as the restaurant today can be traced to 18th century France. The French were the first to introduce the menu to the dining experience, creating a style of service known as 'a la carte'.

Before the 18th century, Europeans only ate in public gatherings during ceremonies and special events. While most meals were prepared at home by peasants and farmers, travellers often dined in lodges along popular trade routes. Here lodging, wine, beer and food were the only comforts of the road. Instead of a menu, the food served reflected the local availability for the day. The pre-18th century meal consisted of bread and some sort of stew. The stew included broth, vegetables and meat.

While travel defined the European 'restaurant' prior to the 18th century, Constantinople was known for its coffee houses as early at the 16th century. Here, travellers and locals alike would meet to discuss politics, city life, travel, philosophy and religions. In fact, early Constantinople introduced the term, 'café' to the world.

Formal dining was refined by the French prior to the French revolution. Grand meals were prepared by highly skilled chefs at French courts such as Versailles. Intricate pastries, long roasted meats and premium sauce-work defined these bountiful meals. And with the words of Marie Antoinette, "Let them eat cake", the French revolution was born. Soon, the skilled chefs of the royal court were in need of work and transitioned to more public enterprises. Restaurants such as Boulanger and Grande Taverne de Londres sprung up around the streets of Paris, ushering in the modern era of the restaurant.

Soon, the formality of the French meal became the rage of London, Berlin, Moscow, Rome and the developing city of New York. While the well-to-do were being catered for, entrepreneurs quickly realized the potential of this dining environment. Pubs and saloons began to spring up to serve the working class. The future of the restaurant was secure.

Restaurant concepts became heavily diverse towards the beginning of the 20th century. Italian cuisine was brought to the New World by means of immigrants. The same can be said for German, Irish and Italian cuisines. The new immigrant class created environments where their fellow expatriates could gather to discuss the old world, new cities, borrowing money as well as the other necessary functions of the immigrant life. Then came creativity. Ice cream parlours began to open. The concept of fast food was introduced to the world. Chinese food restaurants opened around the world. The depth and breadth of the restaurant world was truly complex by the turn of the 21st century.

Today, restaurants can be classified into dozens of concepts and categories. Each year, new trends emerge which try to entice the modern day consumer. Healthy lifestyles are changing the way restaurants formulate menus, while the busy life schedule of consumers has reduced the amount of time committed to the dining experience. Technology has changed the way we perceive a restaurant before we choose to dine, making reviews from clients a reality for restaurants today and well into the future.

WHAT MAKES A SUCCESSFUL RESTAURATEUR

There are many factors which make a successful restaurant, and there are many factors which make a successful restaurateur. While the majority of the book explains the elements needed to make a successful restaurant, it is a good idea to spend some time making sure you remember and maintain the elements which make a successful restaurant owner. A restaurant can have the best location or ambiance in a city, but under bad management, even this restaurant can fail. By following a simple list of personal qualities, you will dramatically increase the chances of success in the business.

A Commitment to Quality

All customers expect a quality product, and this is especially true in the restaurant business. In fact, you can cook a steak perfectly nine times in a row for a certain customer, and then loose that customer when his tenth steak is served too well done. This is just the reality of the business. To become very successful in the restaurant business, you need to build a large and loyal clientele. Having a high commitment to quality greatly increases your chances of success.

Quality can mean many things in the restaurant business. For example, the concept of quality in a fine dining restaurant and fast food burger joint will be different. Fine dining requires ingredients which are grass fed, organic, local. Fast food requires ingredients which are fresh and safe. You want to make sure you maintain the quality of your food as it was first presented on your opening day. In other words, you need to remain consistent. A high commitment to quality will go a long way.

Great People Skills

Having great people skills is a vital quality of the restaurateur. You need to make people feel welcome and confident with your presence in order to instil a sense of trust and comfort. To make sure you remain close to your clientele, it is important to remain visible to your customers. A restaurant where the owner is present represents a well-run business.

When interacting with the customers and staff, it's important, always, to be proper and polite. No one likes to be treated poorly when eating out, and this is especially true when dealing with customers. Always smiling while learning to say 'please' and 'thank you' will go a long way in the minds of your customers. If you begin to grow a local clientele, make sure to remember the names of your frequent customers. This will make the customer feel as if they are important part of your business and will help to form a long term business relationship. If a customer has a bad experience at your restaurant, they are very likely to discuss their experience with you directly, giving you valuable insight into your staff as well as the ability to keep a loyal customer. With this said, always be sure to ask your customers for feedback. As a restaurateur, you want to be a great listener. Some of the best restaurant items and concepts were created by owners who took the time to listen to their customers. Finally, make people laugh. Make sure to keep a smile on your customer's faces by telling them a joke or simply smiling. A happy restaurant is a successful restaurant.

Great Money Management Skills

The number one reason restaurants fail can be traced to undercapitalization. Meaning, most restaurants run out of money before they have the opportunity to turn a profit. For this reason, all great restaurateurs have great management skills. Before the doors open, you want to make sure you have enough cash on hand to cover the expenses for an entire business year. Make sure to ask yourself twice before spending money on something which is not essentially required for your restaurant. Having the nicest linens in your city will certainly be appreciated by your customers, but the cost to fit your tables with expensive linens might translate to months of labour and rent. Learning to grow within your budget is the most important factor when it comes to opening a successful restaurant.

Be a Great Organizer

To understand all the aspects of your business model, you need to be a great organizer. The better you organize the books of the business, the better chance you have to understand your expenses and how to limit waste. Saving receipts, invoices and timesheets are some of the obvious ways to remain organized. With this said, organization goes beyond the books. Organizing your kitchen, liquor room, linen closet and promotional materials requires a daily commitment on your part. Make sure to actively look for ways to improve your organization on a daily basis. Building a fast and efficient system will allow you to spend more time completing the more enjoyable tasks of the restaurant business such as tasting wine and eating out.

TODAY'S RESTAURANT TRENDS

Keeping your restaurant concept modern and relevant is especially important when opening a new establishment. In 2013, there are a number of unique and identifiable trends which are sure to gain popularity in all corners of the world. The central theme to restaurants trends is mostly driven by the economic downturn. High priced, formal restaurants were replaced in popularity by lower costing, relaxed restaurants. In the coming years, you are likely to see the following types becoming rather more popular and trendy.

Mixologists and Cocktail Driven Bars

Fancy and highly involved cocktails are all the rage these days. The added degree of creativity and art in the area of cocktails has given way to the mixologist. A mixologist is someone who employs modern techniques to create inventive cocktails. Many times, this includes making in-house ingredients such bitters and tonic. Lesser known alcohols, especially local and small batch distilleries are highly used by the mixologist. Creating a restaurant with an advanced bar program can increase your profit and foot traffic dramatically.

In-House Soft Drinks

While Coke and Pepsi has dominated the soft drink business for nearly a century, a new movement has taken off which involves the creation of in-house sodas. Here, the restaurant creates rich and flavoursome syrups, which are then combined with water and carbon dioxide. The recipe is bottled and served to the restaurant crowd. This is a great way to create a unique concept as well as also creating a retail item to sell in your restaurant. With homemade soft drinks, the potential for profit can be found outside the walls of the restaurant. With this said, you can further expand your enterprise outside the walls of the restaurant. Packaged sauces, ground coffees, specialty teas and smoothies are just a few potential concepts to add to your external portfolio.

Premium Quick Service

While the global financial downturn has changed the formality of the restaurant industry, consumers still demand high quality ingredients and creative recipe concoctions. For this reason, when consumers eat a cheeseburger, they want high quality beef, cheese, bread and crisps. Consumers are also keen on eating high quality ethnic foods in quick service settings. For this reason, consider opening a premium quick service restaurant.

Artisan Snack Food Shops

Consumers are looking for meals which are not only made with organic ingredients but are homemade. In artisan snack food shops, breads are made at the store, crisps are cut from potatoes and fried in the shop and the ketchup is typically a signature recipe from the shop. Not only does this mentality play to the wants and desires of the modern food consumer, artisan food shops are well-positioned to bring their food products to retail stores. For instance, if the signature ketchup recipe is a tremendous success, it becomes rather easy to produce this recipe in a commissary industrial kitchen.

Technology Driven Menus

Technology is all the rage in restaurants today. A new and emerging trend is to use iPads or other tablets to share menus, place orders and give the customer a unique user experience. By hiring a computer scientist or designer, you can create a unique and compelling technology driven menu. The benefit of technology goes beyond the menu. Social media, a powerful driver of new customers, can benefit your restaurant greatly.

Nutrition

The modern consumer requires a healthy meal nowadays. When major chains in the United States were forced to publish the nutrition of their foods on the menu, these companies were surprised when sales for such items reach 40% of total sales. For this reason, formulating a nutritionally-minded menu will certainly increase your traffic significantly.

Locally Focused Food

With global warming being a popular and passionate issue, many restaurants have turned to local sources of ingredients to reduce their carbon footprint. Not only do locally focused menus help the environment, but they also help the local economy by supporting local farmers. Make sure to take time to contact local farmers and farmer's markets. By integrating their products into your menu, you will gain a powerful and loyal local clientele.

Research, Research, Research

Before you decided to open the cheque book and start a company, you need to conduct tons and tons of research. For a start, it's important to build a map of restaurant competition in your area before you make any significant decisions when it comes to your restaurant concept. For instance, if there are four pizza shops in your desired location, there is no point adding to the mix with your own version of pizza. At the same time, you do not want to open a restaurant with a concept that is too specific. Instead, you want to find one which is <u>underserved</u> in your area. Meaning, you need to find a concept that will be popular with the local clientele, but where you cannot find too many other restaurants which also serve this segment. To find such concepts, a great trick is to discover the foods of a major city such as London, New York and Paris. Determine which new concepts are popular and trendy, and bring this concept to a smaller, secondary city or market. This strategy assures your concept will be popular and underserved.

Beyond concept, there are many factors of the restaurant you want to research before making any critical decisions. A great place to start is by looking at the fixed costs of your potential business. A fixed cost is a monthly or weekly expense which does not change from invoice period to invoice period. For instance, fixed costs in a restaurant are often for rent, a mortgage, labour costs, utility costs and permits. When researching fixed costs, make sure to pay attention to the going rate for restaurant spaces in your area, as well as the average cost for cooks, servers, sommeliers and so on. By knowing these costs up front, it will be much easier to build a convincing business plan when the time arrives.

Beyond fixed costs, it's important to research the local laws associated with opening restaurants. As an example, some European cities limit the number of restaurant permits within the limits of the jurisdiction. You do not want to spend £100,000 on opening your restaurant, only to find you are ineligible for a permit. Also, the local municipality will have very specific rules in regards to alcohol service. Knowing these limits can greatly affect the type and style of restaurant you open. To cover all these possibilities, hire a local legal representative who is well versed in restaurant and food industry law. You will most likely need legal advice to assist with the formalities of opening your business, so seeking out such a specialist will help you tremendously in the months to come.

Among the important issues to consider when conducting your initial research, make sure to spend a good amount of time on the marketing and branding aspects of your business. For instance, start thinking of great names for your restaurant. Ask family and friends for assistance too, for the best restaurant names often come from the most unexpected places. Once you have found a great restaurant name, make sure to research if anyone has used the name before. Check domain hosts such as *GoDaddy* to see if the website name of your restaurant has been taken or is for sale. This will help when it comes time to share your restaurant with the world at large.

Finally, make sure to research how much time you will need to commit to the business before making any major expenses. If you can only commit five hours a week to your restaurant, it might be best to wait a few years until you can firmly commit more time. An absentee owner tends to accelerate a restaurant's failure, so a firm time commitment to your restaurant is one of the most important elements of financial success.

BUILDING YOUR BUSINESS PLAN

When entering the restaurant industry, your business plan serves as the roadmap to the operation and future of your business. Building a proper business plan not only provides direction in the day-to-day financials, but allows you to identify many of the important topics mentioned in this book. You will learn positives from your business plan, but you will also get a heightened sense of the downfalls of your concept. Above all, a well-written business plan is likely to make a larger pool of investors eager to give you money. If you have enough cash to open your dream restaurant, some might say you do not need a business plan. However, self-financed restaurants should always write a business plan in order to judge the success and long term practicality of the business.

When speaking with successful restaurateurs, the most critical step when it came to running their business was the successful implementation of their business plan. With a well-written plan, they are able to grow and maintain their business with a high degree of financial accuracy. This is especially true of restaurants consisting of multiple owners. Sometimes, even a financially successful restaurant will close when partners do not see eye-to-eye on the day-to-day operations of the business. By having a clear and concise document, which lists the rights and responsibilities of all stakeholders, there will be little confusion even years down the road.

A well-written business plan goes beyond the financials of the restaurant. Instead, a well written business plan requires marketing, branding and operational details.

After you have researched names for your business and committed to this name, it's important to secure the domain name as well as begin the branding process. Branding includes creating a logo, social media pages as well as a creative marketing plan. Including these elements in your business plan will not only make your document look good, it will demonstrate to investors that many of the basic tasks have been taken care of. Investors will note that you will be able to open your doors quickly once you receive the funds, assuring they receive a timely return on their investment.

The most important goal you should consider when writing your restaurant business plan is to convey the information in a precise, organised and logical manner. You also want to make sure the content is well-written and grammatically correct. Once you finalise your business plan, it's a good idea to have a professional writer to review the plan for content and grammar.

Executive Summary

The first part of your business plan should be the Executive Summary. Typically one to four pages in length, the executive summary introduces your concept to perspective investors. While this document is found at the beginning of your business plan, make sure to write the executive summary after you have completed the remainder of the plan. By writing this summary at the end of the process, you will gain a great guide to writing a clear and concise summary at the beginning.

A well-written executive summary conveys your restaurant's identity and identifies why it will be a successful business venture. In addition to costs, it is important to add the anticipated return on investment early in the summary. This way, potential investors will see the potential profit instead of the mountain of expenses you expect to take on during the opening process. Make sure to avoid an overly detailed executive summary. If you add too many specific details, most investors will tend to skip over important and convincing aspects of your argument. Finally, it is always a good idea to add a confidentiality statement before the executive summary starts. It would be a shame to see someone take your concept and present it as their own.

Company Description

The next section of the business plan will cover the individual topics of your restaurant concept. To help to make it easier to navigate and understand, it is best to organize your company description into a number of well-organized bullet points. Some of the topics you want to include are:

1. Legal Arrangement of Business.

>   To start, it is best to describe the legal structure of ownership and responsibility. This includes incorporating your business or establishing a Limited Liability Company. If there will be a number of owners, the best method of legal organization is incorporation. Through corporations, owners can exchange shares of the restaurant with ease, allowing partners to leave the business if tensions arise. Incorporating your restaurant is also a great idea if you plan on opening more than one restaurant in the future. This

is especially true for restaurant concepts which plan on franchising their business formula. If you dream big and plan on shelling your shares on a public market, incorporation is also your best bet. If you plan on being a sole owner or will run the business with a family, a Limited Liability Company is the easiest and most efficient type of legal arrangement. Make sure to discuss your individual needs with your legal adviser before settling on a legal business arrangement.

2. Restaurant Lease or Purchase.

The restaurant business is one of the most location sensitive endeavours. For this reason, investors tend to look at the location of the restaurant very carefully. While leasing a space tends to be cheaper in the short term, owning the restaurant and land can be attractive to many investors. Owning the property demonstrates that the value of the property will most likely increase in time. Investors also feel that the collateral of the property helps to offset any worry or risk found in other areas of the business model. With this said, you are unlikely to own or lease a property before writing your business plan. For this reason, you should make clear whether you intend to buy or lease the property. Also, make sure to include comparable prices for both leasing and buying options in your area.

3. Capitalization needs.

Capitalization needs includes the amount of money you expect to need to open the restaurant. As a common practice in the restaurant business, plan on doubling the amount of money you think you will need to open the restaurant. In addition to initial capital expenses, you will also need to consider your expenses for the first twelve months. Calculate the cost of all fixed costs for the first year and add this to your capitalization estimate. For an investor, this number represents the most important financial figure, so make sure to spend a lot of time calculating this value. Keep this section short and to the point. Add the detailed projections in the 'Investment Analysis and Projections' section of your business plan.

4. Business Concept.

While your business plan to this point might seem boring and overly mathematical, completing the concept section of your plan is perhaps the most satisfying. Here, you will be able to form a convincing argument as to why your restaurant idea will be more successful than others. Make sure to portray your argument with passion, painting a descriptive picture of your goals.

While the financial aspects of your business plan are important to potential investors, they are mostly interested in why your restaurant concept is a great idea. Articulating this point will go a long way with investors. Some topics you want to cover when describing your restaurant include:

- ✓ Style of Service (fine dining, quick service, casual, etc.)
- ✓ Ambiance and Décor
- ✓ Seating Capacity

- ✓ Operating Hours
- ✓ Menu Theme
- ✓ Unique Selling Points
- ✓ Related Sales (Catering, Delivery, Retail, etc.)

5. Sample menu
===

Within the company description, you need to include a sample menu for your restaurant. A well-written and interesting menu design will help to attract investors through their stomachs. Since customers view the menu as the most important consideration when choosing a restaurant, it is important to showcase a relevant sample menu. Make sure to add prices to your sample menu to give the investors a sense of potential profit margins. A sample menu also helps to showcase the style of food you plan on selling. Formal restaurants will have lengthy and descriptive menus while fast casual restaurant menus will be short and to the point.

6. Restaurant Design and Layout
===

Beyond the food and financials, investors will want to gain a great sense of what the space will look like on opening day. To make a convincing and visual argument, try to include architectural drawings of your restaurant concept. Floor plans, kitchen layouts and artistic renderings are all positive elements to add to your business plan.

7. Restaurant Management Team Overview

A successful restaurant is not only judged by competent owners, but also judged by competent management. In order to verify your business plan is being successfully implemented, experienced managers need to be placed in positions of authority. Sometimes, the ownership of a restaurant has a tremendous amount of experience. Other times, the ownership is new to the business and requires a few people to assist with the day to day tasks of management. Either way, implementing a competent management team is absolutely necessary in the restaurant business. Remember, it is extremely important to remember that good ownership should not be confused with good management. The owner may have the highest level of authority in the business and restaurant concept, but the owner also has the responsibility to make sure the management is detail-oriented when it comes to running the day to day tasks of the restaurant. For this reason, the managers need to be competent and well structured.

To assure investors you have developed a successful team, it is a good idea to include the following elements to your management team overview:

- ✓ Management Organizational Chart
- ✓ CVs and Biographies of Managers
- ✓ Management Contracts for the Restaurant
- ✓ Financial Incentives for Managers

Restaurant Environment Analysis

Restaurant Environment Analysis is the section of your restaurant business plan which seeks to study the competitive landscape of your market. There are four areas of concentration when writing a restaurant environment analysis:

1. Study Restaurant Trends and Consumer Habits
2. Identify your Target Market
3. Location Analysis
4. Competitive Analysis

Restaurant Marketing Strategy

A successful restaurant business plan always includes a well-written marketing plan. Investors want to know that you have a well thought-out plan for short term and long-term growth. When formulating a successful marketing strategy, you need to paint a picture that details your actions before and after the opening. Make sure to distinguish these two marketing goals. Some great ways to build a compelling marketing strategy include:

1. Build a Customer Database for Direct Marketing
2. Create a Frequent Diner and VIP Programme
3. Develop a Compelling Email Campaign
4. Promote a Direct Mail Campaign for Your Local Postcode
5. Community Involvement such as Charity Events

6. Create T-shirts, Hats, Bumper Stickers, Business Cards
7. Hire a Public Relations Firm for Media Outreach
8. Include an Advertising Budget

Restaurant Operations Plan

The operations plan within your business plan is the largest section of the document. Here, you want to convey the general day to day aspects of your operation. While you might not be able to add every detail of your day to day operations to your business plan, it is important to cover the general tasks you will complete. For instance, you will need a labour schedule for your business, so make sure to add a labour schedule to your business plan, which reflects your intended hours of operation.

To correctly formulate your operations plan, you will need to document the system of controls you will implement in order to hit your financial targets and projections. A few topics you will need to cover in your operations plan include:

- ✓ Staff Structure
- ✓ Employee Training Manual
- ✓ Suppliers
- ✓ Management Controls
- ✓ Point of Sales System
- ✓ Expected Labour Schedule
- ✓ Time and Attendance Tracking

- ✓ Inventory Control Method
- ✓ Insurance and Liability Controls
- ✓ Administrative Controls
- ✓ Cash Controls
- ✓ Weekly Profit/Loss Statement
- ✓ Method of Bookkeeping
- ✓ Payroll Processing

FIRST FINANCIALS

While you will cover many financial numbers in your business plan, there are a few key financial measures you will always need to consider when forming your business concept. Firstly, you need to be able to quickly judge the potential profit margin for your concept as well as the competition. In the restaurant business, profit margins generally range anywhere from 10% to 20%. On average, expect a profit margin of 15% when formulating your business plan.

While it is easy to estimate a profit margin, creating a formula which hits your desired profit margin can be rather difficult. First, you need to know the cost of each menu item. Second, you need to understand your fixed costs. Thirdly, you need to understand the cost of labour needed to create and serve the dishes. Finally, you need to know the cost of each ingredient used.

The best way to hit your desired profit margin is to start with the fixed costs. Determine how many people will eat in your restaurant over the course of a month and divide this number by the total value of fixed costs. This will give you a figure for the fixed cost per guest. Next, calculate the cost of each ingredient and apply this information to determine the cost of each menu item. Finally, determine the labour cost needed to create and serve the dish. Add these three costs and add 30% to the total calculated cost. This calculation will give you a very good estimate in terms of what you should charge customers for each item.

Another important first financial you need to consider is the average price per person. This essential value will give you a sense of how many people will be able to afford to eat at your restaurant. If you plan on serving a lot of people quickly, you need to make sure you have a low average price per person. If you plan on opening a fine dining restaurant, the average price per person should be higher. To establish an average price per person, first determine how many courses the customer will consume at your restaurant. For most restaurants, it's a good idea to use the three course model, consisting of an appetizer, main course and dessert. Using the calculations you used to determine your profit margin, figure out the average cost of an appetizer, main course and dessert. Add these three costs. Next, account for wine and beverages. Most fine dining restaurants gain 50% of their income from wine and beverages, so double the previous calculation to determine your average cost per person. With this data, you can target the correct audience.

While there are many financials to consider when opening a restaurant, understanding your profit margin and average cost per person will give you the most fundamental sense of your future. By finding the correct balance, you can make a lot of money in the restaurant business. If you are too greedy with the profit margin, you will not build a long term, loyal clientele. If you are too liberal with the company cheque book, you will soon be out of business. For this reason, understanding these two measures early on in the process will help you tremendously while you are formulating your business plan.

FINDING FUNDING (INVESTORS)

There are a number of ways to find funding for your restaurant concept. From traditional banks to modern day lenders, it is always a good idea to approach a wide variety of potential money sources. After you have finished your business plan, it is time to approach people in order to gain the necessary financing for your restaurant. To start, try asking friends and family if they are interested in investing in your restaurant. While you are unlikely to find £100,000 investors within your family, you might find a few people close to you who are willing to stake £5,000 on your success. Find 20 such friends and you already have a significant backing. This will certainly help when finding additional investors.

Beyond family and friends, a great way to gain financing for your project is through crowd funding. Websites such as *Kickstarter* were formed to allow people to give money to concepts which benefit a community or bring a new innovation to the world. Many times, restaurant concepts are funded through such crowd funding sources.

Banks are another source for restaurant financing, although it is becoming more and more difficult to convince these institutions to give you money for opening a restaurant.

Banks understand that nearly 90% of restaurants close in the first year, so the chances of recouping their investment are rather low. With this said, banks are more willing to lend you money to open a restaurant if you include collateral in your agreement. Collateral can include your home, cars and other property. At the same time, you might not want to stake your entire life on the success of your restaurant. For this reason, it is never a good idea to stake your home on the success of the business. Beyond banks, venture capitalists are a source of funding. If you have a restaurant concept which can be franchised easily, you are more likely to attract venture capitalists as investors in your restaurant.

The best way to open a restaurant, with the option which will give you the most financial freedom, is to open the restaurant with your personal savings. To eliminate expenses, open a fully renovated restaurant which requires little initial investment. Open a business as well as a couple credit accounts. When cash is limited, transfer money from your savings to your business account. As you become successful and profitable, you can keep 100% of the proceeds; the ultimate satisfaction when opening a restaurant.

Section [2]

Correctly Formulating a Food Service Concept

Beyond the financials of opening a food service concept, there are a number of aspects you need to consider in great depth. To help you to correctly cover all the basics of restaurant concept formulation, the following chapter will help tremendously. Here, we cover the types and styles or restaurants, formalities, alcohol service, architecture, marketing and so on. By learning these basics, you will be able to create a compelling restaurant concept for any style of food service.

THE TYPES AND STYLES OF RESTAURANTS

When it comes to opening a restaurant, it seems as though there are thousands and thousands of types and styles to choose from. With this said, you will need to identify two major factors when choosing a type and style of restaurant to open. The first factor deals with the type of restaurant. Examples include fast food, sit down, formal, and theatric dining, to name a few types of restaurants. The second factor you want to identify relates to the type of cuisine you should serve. To make this process a bit easier to conquer, the following list of concept types and food regions might help a bit:

> **Formal Dining:** Formal dining restaurants are the most expensive restaurants to eat in. With this said, they are also the most expensive restaurants to open. Formal dining includes proper linens, sturdy tables, formal service, fancy plates and expensive glassware. Do not attempt to open a fine dining restaurant unless you have considerable financial backing.

> **Take-Away /Automat:** An automat or take-away restaurant is one where there is very little interaction between the customers and staff. The staff are typically hidden behind a wall which contains the foods for sale. In order to purchase the foods, the customer places money in a slot and a door opens. Out pops the food, cold or hot. This type of restaurant has the lowest labour cost of all restaurant types.

> **Bakery:** A bakery is a restaurant which concentrates on the production of breads, desserts, simple sandwiches and salads.

> **Bar/Pub:** A pub or bar is a type of restaurant which mostly sells alcohol and beer. Food is not the focus of most pubs and bars, but a great bar menu can increase traffic and sales dramatically.

Cafeteria: A cafeteria is a type of restaurant where the customer chooses foods from large buffet tables. The foods selected by the customer are placed on a tray and paid for at the end of the buffet line. The customer brings their tray to a table and eats their meal after paying for it at the cash desk. Cafeterias tend to sell a very diverse set of foods.

Café / Bistro: The most common and popular style of restaurant, a café or bistro is a very comfortable restaurant space and includes a waiter or waitress. Formality is not very common in this type of restaurant, making them especially popular among younger crowds.

Coffeehouse: A coffeehouse is a restaurant type which focuses on the production and sale of coffee, tea and snacks. Since coffee is a relatively cheap ingredient, coffeehouses can have rather impressive profit margins.

> **Drive-In**: A drive in restaurant is a concept where the customer drives their car onto the restaurant property. The customer orders food from the car window, and a server brings the meal to the car. This style of restaurant was very popular in 1960s America. Drive-In restaurants, such as McDonalds, are popular today in the UK.

Fast Food/ Quick Service: Fast food is a type of restaurant which focuses on a low wait time for food. This style of restaurant is a no frills adventure. Service is low and the cost of the meals are typically low.

Food Cart: A food cart is perhaps the cheapest type of restaurant to open. Since there is no physical space to decorate and equip, you will find it easy to open a food cart. Even better, a food cart allows you to travel to where your customers are likely to be.

Delicatessen: A deli is a type of restaurant which focuses on sandwich and catering sales. Deli's are very popular in business districts since they attract a rather large lunch crowd.

Diner: Diners are perhaps the most diverse type of restaurant. Diners sell a variety of cuisine styles, from Italian to Asian. In addition, diners tend to serve their entire menu throughout the day. Breakfast can be had late at night, or dinner can be enjoyed early in the morning.

Supper Club: A supper club is a type of restaurant which is becoming more and more popular. Instead of being a highly public and trafficked site, a supper club is typically barely visible to the outside world. Instead, a supper club relies on a good reputation of pleasure seeking foodies. Because of this, supper clubs tend to have low rents, making them attractive to many restaurateurs.

Theme Restaurant: A themed restaurant is a style of food service which includes a fictional element to the ambiance. For instance, a German restaurant which features music and entertainment throughout the night is considered a theme restaurant. Theme restaurants tend to be very popular with young families, especially when they include a cartoon like atmosphere.

Culinary Cultures by Region

The number of regional food cultures found around the world is certainly immense. While you might be set on a particular style of cuisine to feature in your restaurant, it is always a good idea to consider alternative and unique styles of food to add to your menu. To give you an overview of global cuisines, the following should help:

Asian cuisine

Ingredients common to many cultures in the east and southeast regions of the continent include rice, ginger, garlic, sesame seeds, chilies, dried onions, soy, and tofu. Additionally, cooking methods such as stir frying, steaming and deep frying are common. While rice is common to most Asian cuisines, different varieties are popular in the different regions. Basmati rice is popular in the subcontinent while Jasmine rice is found across Southeast Asia. Long-grain rice is popular in China while short-grain is popular in Japan and Korea. Since Asian cuisine varies widely, opening an Asian themed restaurant is sure to attract a large percentage of the local population.

Chinese cuisine

Chinese restaurants have become tremendously popular around the world. Being a culturally diverse country, there are many types of Chinese cuisines. With this said, there are eight main regional types of Chinese foods, also known as the Eight Great Traditions: Anhui, Cantonese, Fujian, Hunan, Jiangsu, Shandong, Sichuan and Zhejiang. Among them, Cantonese, Sichuan, Shandong are often considered as the standouts of Chinese cuisine and due to their influence. By studying the vast complexity of Chinese food, you are sure to create a unique and compelling Chinese restaurant.

Southeast Asian cuisine

Southeast Asian cuisines include lightly prepared dishes with strong aromatic components and herbs such as mint, cilantro and basil. Fish sauce is commonly used instead of soy sauce, while tamarind and lemongrass remain popular ingredients. Curry dishes are popular and typically consist of the spices cardamom, cumin, coriander and star anise. While Thai food seems to be the most popular of southeast Asian cuisines, Vietnamese and Cambodian restaurants remain highly sought after concepts in smaller city markets.

Indian cuisine

Indian cuisine is characterized by its sophisticated use of spices and vegetables. Considered by some to be one of the world's most diverse cuisines, Indian cuisine is characterized by a wide assortment of dishes and cooking techniques. As a consequence, Indian cuisine varies from region to region, reflecting the varied demographics of the country.

India's religious practices and culture have played an influential role in the evolution of its food. However, cuisine across India also evolved with the subcontinent's interactions with the Middle East, Central Asia and the Mediterranean. Colonial India introduced European cooking styles to India adding to its flexibility and diversity. Indian restaurants are very popular in the United Kingdom.

Middle Eastern Cuisine

Middle Eastern cuisine is defined as the various cultures spanning the Arab World from Iraq to Morocco. The styles of food have been influenced to a degree by the cuisines of Turkey, Pakistan, Rome, Iran, India and the Mediterranean. Middle Eastern food is heavily spiced and generally remains strict to Halal standards. Nuts and dried fruits are very popular, as well as cous cous. When opening a Middle Eastern restaurant, you can choose to focus on one type of regional food and create a menu which reflects the diverse recipes of the Arab people.

European cuisine

European cuisine, also known as Western cuisine, is a generalized term collectively referring to the food cultures of the European continent. The most popular European styles of food are French and Italian, while Spanish and Greek influences are major components of the regional identity. While spices were imported to Europe, most regional variations are based on the climate from which fruits and vegetables could grow. For this, the foods of Northern France vary greatly from the foods found on the southern tip of Spain. English food is considerably influenced by the exotic ingredients of its colonies. Tea is perhaps the greatest example of this colonial condition. Dutch food is influenced by colonies as well, although the colonial identities are mainly Thailand and Suriname. German food is a popular style of restaurant in the United States. This can be traced to the high number of immigrants who moved to America in the 19th Century. For this reason, Italian restaurants and Irish pubs are also popular around the world.

American cuisine

The food identity of the United States dates back before the colonial period when Native Americans had a rich and diverse cooking style for an equally diverse amount of ingredients. With the arrival of Europeans, the style of cookery changed vastly, with numerous ingredients introduced from Europe, as well as cooking styles and modern cookbooks. The style of cookery continued to expand into the 19th and 20th centuries with the influx of immigrants from various nations across the world. This influx has created a rich diversity and a unique regional character throughout the country. For this reason, American restaurants tend to be defined by the cuisines of the world. Beyond this rich tradition, America is known for inventing Fast Food and Quick Service concepts. McDonalds is perhaps the most popular and well known of American fast food restaurants.

South America

South America is a very diverse food Continent. In Peru, the food is strongly influenced by Incan cuisine. In Patagonia, lamb, beef and venison are major food staples. Tuna and tropical fish are caught all around the continent, while river fish add to the diversity of regional menus. Fruit, including citrus, mango and papaya are abundant in this region. Chiles and herbs add to the diversity of the regions cuisine, with a bountiful array of recipes being both spicy and complex in taste. With vast natural resources, South America enjoys a very vast network of ingredients and cooking techniques. For this reason, South American food makes a great foundation for any restaurant.

Caribbean cuisine

Caribbean food is a fusion of West African, French, Dutch, Spanish, Indian and British foods. These traditions were brought from the many homelands of this region's population. Seafood is one of the most common foods found in the islands along with chicken and lamb. Citrus is often used in the foods of the Caribbean along with spices and herbs. Rice, beans, yam and jicama are commonly consumed starches of the region. Curries are also an important part of Caribbean cuisines.

African cuisine

African cuisine in general would refer to cuisines of sub Saharan Africa and tend to exclude the North African Cuisine, which is generally related to Arabic or even Mediterranean cuisines. Even within Sub Saharan Africa, the main distinctions are generally divided into East and Southern, characterized by steamed or boiled carbohydrates such as bananas, tubers, in spicing and heavier use of hot pepper, but grilled meats, stews and shallow fried dishes. Fresh water fish such as Tilapia are popular. Generally is known to be heavy on flavour but mild in terms of spiciness. The West African region may be related to Caribbean distinctive as many dishes are fused, such as five meats to make up a stew. Accompaniments of carbohydrates and side dishes are typical of all the sub-Saharan African regional cuisine.

Beyond regional taste preferences, it is important to identify the type of restaurant you want to open. If you want to open a Chinese restaurant, ask yourself if you want to open a formal Chinese restaurant or a quick service

Chinese restaurant. While the food might appear the same, the business model of a formal and quick service restaurant can be quite different. For this reason, we have spent a bit of time discussing the types of restaurants.

Formality

In terms of formality, there are a few restaurant types you need to consider. For one, fine dining tends to have the most formal atmosphere. For this reason, if you plan on opening a fine dining restaurant, make sure to precisely identify your style of formality. While fast casual and quick service restaurants do not require a system of formality, you might want to integrate a concept or two into your café or bistro concept.

French service is considered the most formal of services. For one, the staff is proactive and detail oriented. In French fine dining, the food is brought to the table by the staff and placed in front of the guest. With this said, the occasional French dish is prepared in front of the audience. There is a proper way to serve guests wine and courses are served in a particular order. For this reason, if you plan on opening a restaurant under the French style of service, it is best to hire a very knowledgeable Maître D.

Even if you open an Indian restaurant, it is a good idea to pay attention to the formalities used in a French bistro or café. For instance, you should always serve a customer on the left and remove dishes from the right. Female guests should always be served before the male customers, and customers should feel comfortable asking for special requests. Since the French style of formality is the most popular in the world, make sure to integrate this style into your restaurant concept if formality is required.

QUICK SERVICE VERSUS SIT DOWN SERVICE

A quick service meal versus a sit-down restaurant meal are very different experiences. For one, a sit down restaurant requires you to invest heavily in tables, chairs, silverware, glassware - as well as hire front of house staff. As you can imagine, the expenses can add up quickly. A sit down restaurant also requires a large dining room since customers tend to sit and eat for longer periods of time. For this reason, it is important to understand whether or not your location is well suited for a slow meal. Otherwise, you might consider opening a quick service restaurant.

Quick service restaurants are becoming more and more popular. Restaurant customers do not have the time to commit to a two hour meal anymore, nor do they have the money to spend on elaborate dishes and service. Quick service restaurants generally require less of an investment when compared to full service establishments. Instead of formal linens, a quick service restaurant will serve food in cheap disposable products which are heavily branded with the restaurant logo. Chairs and tables can be made from cheaper materials, while owners can fit more customers into a smaller space. Enticing visuals and clear, concise menu descriptors are paramount to attract customers as well as providing quick service and decision making. For this reason, many new restaurateurs today are of the quick service variety. Understanding the time and cost constraints of your demographic will certainly help you choose the correct path when it comes to quick service versus sit down restaurant concepts.

TAKE AWAY OR DELIVER TO THEM

While formal restaurant do not typically allow take away or delivery, a number of restaurant types can benefit greatly from this sort of customer interaction. Firstly, consumers with families or busy schedules can eat their favourite foods on the go or while multitasking. There is no sense in turning away business, so creating a take-away menu is a great addition to any restaurant.

Delivery can be a tricky endeavour for any restaurant. Some restaurants hire an employee or employees whose sole purpose is to deliver food. When you first open your restaurant, you might not want to hire someone to fill a position with an unknown result. For this reason, try using a member of the clearing up or assisting staff as your delivery person at first. As you become busier and drive more delivery traffic, you can hire a delivery person as needed.

ALCOHOL / BAR SERVICE

Serving alcohol in your restaurant will certainly increase overall sales. However, getting a liquor or alcohol license can be a difficult process, requiring permits and approvals from local and regional councils. Liquor is typically taxed, adding another headache to your business plan. If you plan on opening a full service restaurant, you will certainly need to obtain a liquor license. However, if you plan on opening a quick service restaurant, you might consider opening without alcohol. Not only will this make your business plan simpler, it will eliminate unwanted late night traffic.

Fine and Formal dining are also usually associated with accompaniment of fine wines or ales. Themed restaurants and other set ups are well complimented by the wine and alcohol selections and they can become an element of attraction to the experience at the establishment. So, it is important to find the correct type and styles of alcohol to serve in your restaurant.

Studying Competition

There are many ways to study competition in the restaurant industry. For one, you need to pay attention to the restaurants which are closest to your desired location. Study the types of cuisine and try to differentiate from these. Study the cost per person and make sure to fit within this range. Make sure to pay attention to slogans, logo and marketing materials to determine which techniques work best in the local arena. Beyond your local competition, you should spend some time getting to know your global competition. For instance, if you are opening a quick service restaurant, make sure to study the types of quick service restaurants becoming more and more popular around the globe. By knowing these competitive benchmarks, you will be able to create a compelling concept which resonates with the local population. If viable, try to travel to a few cities to get a sense of the menus and flavours of similar restaurant concepts to your own.

Studying competition does not exclusively relate to the physical traits of a restaurant. Today, understanding how your competition uses social media remains an important pillar of all new restaurants. Follow your competitors on *Facebook* and *Twitter* to comprehend how they reach their customers with daily deals and menu specials. By studying your competitor's social behaviour, you can quickly tap into their well of loyal customers. In many ways, competition provides the path to opening a successful restaurant concept.

AMBIANCE AND ARCHITECTURE

Besides the food, the ambiance and environment of your restaurant is exceptionally important. If your restaurant is uncomfortable or too noisy, you are sure to lose a large group of potential customers. With this said, most new restaurants require a high degree of design and development. At the very least, you should make sure to choose a compelling colour for the walls of your restaurant. Fill the walls and corners with items and colours which complement the room and make it feel comfortable and relaxing. To assure your design fits your restaurant concept, try hiring an interior designer. Knowing your budget, an interior designer will know how to get the greatest impact for your money. Remember, one great opportunity for your upscale or trendy restaurant includes preferred seating and/or VIP sections. This can help to upsell your restaurant significantly.

If you plan on doing extensive renovations in your restaurant, it is always a good idea to hire an architect. Large renovations require permits and inspections, and an architect will be able to best manage this process. Make sure to choose an architect with extensive restaurant experience.

IDENTIFYING FUNCTIONS OF THE RESTAURANT SPACE, FINE DINING OR PARTYING

As you map the layout of your restaurant, make sure to account for secondary functions of the business. For instance, if you plan on having an extensive catering business, it might be a good idea to add additional kitchen and refrigerator space to your business plan and layout designs. If you plan on opening a fine dining restaurant, make sure to leave room for a linen press, coat check as well as room to store glassware and wine. If you plan on serving large parties on a nightly basis, you might decide to choose a restaurant space with private dining rooms. You also need to consider the logistics of your operation. For instance, you do not want to be carrying deliveries through the dining room, so make sure to account for deliveries during normal business hours using a different route.

Every restaurant has a unique layout which requires a unique plan. To make this process easy to understand, it is best to identify functions of your business. Identify these functions and list them on a piece of paper. As you study the design plans for your restaurant, make sure that each function can be accomplished with the current design plans. Some of these functions include the positioning of the bar, displays, areas for group parties, etc. If not, it might be a good idea to change your plans or find a new restaurant location.

MARKETING AND BRANDING

Consumers tend to accept or reject a restaurant before they even give the food a chance. Instead, the first 'food' a consumer tastes can be traced to the marketing and branding of your restaurant. For this reason, it is very important to invest in a convincing marketing and branding campaign. To start, build your brand. You want to focus on creating a compelling name and logo for your business. From here, create unique and memorable ways of selling your restaurant concept to the world. Business cards and direct mail flyers are great ways to brand your restaurant to potential consumers.

Marketing your restaurant can be a tricky task to accomplish. Choosing the correct words to describe your restaurant is a lot harder than simply choosing three or four words. Instead, it is important to craft a clear and concise message. Since you only have one shot to reach customers, it is always a good idea to hire a marketing professional before and during your restaurants opening. By hiring a professional, you will find unique ways to reach a large diverse customer base.

Section [3]

Property / Premises: To Buy or To Lease

Choosing the correct location for your restaurant is immensely important. While the High Street might seem like the best way to reach customers, some restaurants have become successful for being off the beaten path. For this reason, it's important to find the balance between what a property costs and the amount of traffic the location receives. When opening a restaurant, a confusing part of the process can be traced to the status of the property; renting or leasing. With these simple notes, it will become easier to make the best decision for your restaurant concept.

Location, Location, Location

The location of your restaurant is a very, very, very important aspect of your business. For quick service restaurants, the busier the area the better. You need a high degree of foot traffic to increase sales. On the other hand, some restaurants do very well when they are not located in busy areas of town. This is particularly true for destination venues where customers come in groups and therefore are likely to be driving, which requires parking spaces. As another example, a town or village known for its rest and relaxation can be a great place to open a restaurant, provided it gets the proper amount of weekend traffic. Determine how many customers you will need on a weekly or daily basis, then compare this data to the traffic you expect for the area. In addition to walk-in traffic, make sure to lure customers to your business through marketing as well. While the location is the most important part of your restaurants success, it's still very important to look beyond location.

The Benefits of Buying a Property

Buying a restaurant is a major financial decision which a long term commitment. If you have limited funds to open your restaurant, you are very unlikely to buy a property. People who buy a restaurant and property have typically been in the restaurant business for a while or have significant capital. The most important factor, along with having a first rate restaurant, is a location's ability to attract customers. An attractive property in a well-travelled area can be a smart investment. However, you need to be meticulous when doing your research. Considering the purchase as a long-term commitment, you need to know that the location has a history of economic stability. You also need to know what the local planning commission has in mind regarding zoning and accessibility.

One advantage to owning the restaurant property is the fact that you will not have to worry about a rent increase. In addition, you do not have to consider the sensitivities of a landlord, allowing you a great degree of business freedom. By building equity in your property, you gain a secure investment which you can borrow against during lean economic years. For many long-term restaurateurs, owning the property is the key to long success.

The Benefits of Leasing Property

Most restaurant owners begin their empire by leasing. This financial arrangement allows new restaurant owners to free up capital for marketing, equipment and architectural additions to their property. As a restaurant grows in popularity, many owners decide to allow their lease to expire and open a restaurant on their own property. While this is a great long term goal, the reality is you will most likely start as a renter.

Before you sign a restaurant lease, it is important to understand what the landlord will and will not allow you to modify. The space needs to have the wiring, ventilation, and plumbing to house a restaurant, and with that in mind, you may or may not need to do some remodelling to bring the facility up to your standards as well as up to code. Be sure to clearly understand which expenses you will be responsible for and what expenses the owner will be responsible for. An experienced landlord will know the potential profits a successful restaurant can bring to their property. The landlord will also know how to utilize the facility to suit your needs. For this reason, it is important to build a good relationship with the landlord.

Parking, entrance, frontage, kitchen, bar location, facilities

Make sure to spend time getting to know the specific needs of your business model. For instance, if you plan on opening a restaurant in the country, having a car park large enough to accommodate your maximum number of clients will be very important. If you are a restaurant which plans on receiving a lot of walk-in business, having a compelling and comforting restaurant frontage will be very important. Beyond tasks which focus on the customer, it is important to consider the needs of the kitchen. Will the cooks have enough room to prep and cook the meals? Do you have enough room to add lockers for the employees? Will there be enough room for dry storage? These are just a few questions you need to ask yourself when planning the layout of your space.

Creative Arrangements

In some cases, the prestige of bringing a well-known restaurant into a prime location can land you a very favorable leasing arrangement and financing. For this reason, if you have enjoyed some amount of fame in the food or celebrity world, make sure to emphasize this fame when it's time to negotiate the lease or business plan. Both landlords and banks are open to these sorts of arrangements, so try to be creative if needed.

Section [4]
The Basics of Running a Restaurant

Working the Business Plan

Now that you have gone through the process of writing a business plan and finding investors, it is time to start building the basics you will need to run your restaurant. As you fulfill more pre-opening tasks, it is important to update your business plan as strategies change. This includes updating your projected profit margin when you finally contact your suppliers and get up to date price quotes. Additionally, make sure to update the financial information when you find your restaurant property. In many ways, you want to treat the business plan as a dynamic guide to opening your restaurant.

It is important to update your investors from time to time in terms of your progress opening the restaurant.

Make sure to inform them of major changes to your financial outlook. It is also important to tell your investors if you have accomplished a task for less money than needed, and how you plan on using these extra funds within the project. Having an open and transparent relationship with your investors will prove beneficial in the long term.

Setting up the operations

To start, you will need to outline the process you will use to open the restaurant. Setting up your operations can be a complex task to manage. There are many major functions you need to accomplish months ahead of the opening, and if you miss these dates, you might delay the opening for months. Months of delays can means months of rent and payments. In fact, many restaurants that fail are restaurants which open well beyond the expected opening date. As the restaurant remains dormant, the cash flow of the restaurant remains dormant as well. Opening your restaurant without liquidity will certainly end as a doomed project. To avoid this fate, make sure to take great care when setting up your operations. Beyond the logistics of the opening, make sure to consider the season of your opening. In some regions, your target audience might only be around for three to six months. For instance, many citizens of the UK take holidays in Spain during the summer. If you open a restaurant in a holiday town out of season, your restaurant will remain dormant until the next season starts.

Within this book, we discuss many types of operations which are essential when opening a restaurant. To start, it is best to clearly write your operational objectives into a well-organized list. Make sure to add each element which is important to your unique restaurant. For instance, a few objectives which you might need to add to your list include:

- ✓ Obtain Liquor or Alcohol Permits
- ✓ Set up Food Suppliers
- ✓ Order Glasses, Plates and Silverware
- ✓ Order Menus
- ✓ Test Recipes
- ✓ Set up Wine Accounts
- ✓ Set up Beverage Accounts
- ✓ Set up Sanitation Accounts
- ✓ Restaurant Kitchen Tasks
- ✓ Restaurant Bar Tasks

By remaining highly organized when it comes to setting up your operation, you will reduce a large amount of stress and worry which many restaurateurs endure during their opening. By the time you finish reading this book, you will have a greater sense of which topics are important to your particular restaurant.

DEALING WITH SUPPLIERS AND PROCUREMENT

One of the most important tasks you need to accomplish during the pre-opening involves the supply of food and goods to your restaurant. All restaurants have multiple suppliers, so it is important to approach the multi-faceted aspect of your business with a high degree of organization.

In terms of food suppliers, you are most likely to have between three and four suppliers at the minimum. Most wholesale suppliers specialize in one category of food, so you will have a Meat Supplier, Fish Supplier, Vegetable Supplier and Dry Goods Supplier. Some restaurants use very large companies which service all these goods, but it is best to stay away from them. Large companies are difficult to negotiate with and tend to sell perishable goods which are not on par with their specialist counterparts.

Companies which supply Dry Goods also supply many other goods. Beyond ketchup, flour and sugar, you can typically order cleaning supplies and kitchen supplies from these companies. For instance, you can order detergent for your dishwasher, pot scrubbers, aluminium foil and paper products. This arrangement can be beneficial, since most Dry Goods companies require a minimum order when it comes to delivering goods. By ordering food and supplies from a Dry Goods company, you can meet the minimum order requirement and eliminate additional deliveries to your door. Meat, fish and produce companies often have minimum orders as well. However, these minimums tend to be rather small, since fresh foods need to be delivered to a restaurant on a daily basis.

Make sure to contact suppliers at least six weeks before you plan on opening. By taking care of this task early, you can dedicate more time to the restaurant as the opening nears. It is always a good idea to interview more than one supplier, so make sure to invite a number of companies to discuss your needs and their abilities. Ask the representative from the company to come to your restaurant for the meeting. They can get a sense of your space and needs, and you can save a lot of travel time. Discuss the line of products they sell, the minimum orders, their delivery days, credit terms, your opening date and contracts. Once your application is approved, you are ready to place your first food orders.

Beyond food suppliers, you need to contact your wine and liquor suppliers well before you open your restaurant. In terms of wine, you are very likely to spend a good deal of time tasting wine with your rep before the opening date. To make sure you have enough time to taste, it is a good idea to contact the wine company at least two months before the opening. Some local governments require that your liquor licence be approved before receiving alcohol from suppliers, so taking care of this task early in the operations process will benefit you greatly.

There are many other suppliers you need to contact when opening your restaurant. Among the additional suppliers, you might consider finding a separate supplier for paper goods. Many specialty packaging companies sell paper goods in bulk rates which can be very attractive, especially if you are opening a fast food or quick service restaurant. These companies can also assist you with the branding of your packaging, giving your restaurant a personal packaging touch. You will also need office supplies as you run your restaurant, so finding a reliable and cost-effective office supplier is important. You will need paper for invoices, tape, pens, calculators, and many other office supplies, so finding a company which can supply these in one day or so is very beneficial. Companies such as Staples also offer great rebates to loyal customers, greatly reducing the cost of supplies to your restaurant.

If you are a fine dining restaurant, you will most likely want to find a linen supply company to launder your napkins and tablecloths. Many companies rent the linens through a contract which includes laundering and replacement. If you are opening a fast food restaurant, you will most likely need a beverage company which sells Coke or Pepsi and other soft drinks in bulk.

Each restaurant has their own unique set of suppliers. To make sure you hire the correct number of suppliers, as well as finding a supplier for EVERY 'ingredient' of the restaurant, carefully track your supply and ingredient inventory lists during the pre-opening. By remaining organized when finding suppliers, you will find the opening of your restaurant a much more peaceful process.

There are aspects of procurement that require your direct oversight and these you will need to personally purchase. Examples include some grades of products or specific spicing or specialty items that may not be deliverable. It's important to remain focused on impeccable organization and the crucial aspect of saving time, the latter being a critical aspect of controlling how properly the organization and management will plan out.

Running everyday activity can be like a roller coaster, once started, you cannot just stop it unless in an emergency. The more organized and structured you are at the beginning, the better.

MANAGEMENT AND PRODUCTION

In order to maintain a steady and quality production, management needs to be present at all times. For instance, you need to make sure a Sous Chef is always present in the kitchen to deal with any unexpected events. It is important to have the bar manager present for at least five days of the week, and the same can be said for the Maître D.

Besides being present yourself, you need to devise ways for management to account for the quality of the production. For instance, if the food cost rises from week to week, it is time to assess the waste being produced in the kitchen. If you are selling less and less wine, it is time to review the procedures for selling wine. If you do not have a way to identify these issues, you will not have a way to correct them. For this reason, it is important to create a system of review which accounts for problems which influence the bottom line.

KEEPING THE AUDITS/ REVIEWS OF DAY RUNNING

When running a restaurant, it is extremely important to keep careful track of your finances. To accomplish this goal without serious problems down the road, make sure to save every receipt to receive and process. If you retain every invoice and receipt, both incoming and outgoing, you can manage your finances no matter what happens. For instance, while technology helps to manage the finances of a restaurant, technology also breaks down from time to time. If this happens, at least you can recover the hard copies of your invoices and receipts. A major headache avoided.

Beyond preserving your records for financial sake, many localities will audit your books from time to time. This is especially true in areas which are prone to alcohol restrictions. For instance, the local liquor authority might come to review your books in order to make sure all of your purchased liquor has been taxed correctly. Not having this information can be a warning sign to these agencies, and might lead to a more detailed inspection by the local revenue service. You want to avoid this at all costs.

Beyond the formalities of record keeping, you will need to maintain your data from daily and weekly audits. For instance, you need to analyze your financial data on a week to week basis. In order to correctly determine the profit or loss for the week, you will need to know the Gross Receipts for the week as well as the cost of goods. By having this information handy and well organized, it becomes easier to put together an accurate picture of your financial state.

MONEY MATTERS, TAKINGS

Handling money in a restaurant must be taken with care. For example, you do not want too many employees being able to handle the money, or you can expect a fair amount of theft. Instead, hold the managers responsible for handling cash. Beyond accepting cash from your guests, you might need to make payments to suppliers via cash. In this case, a petty cash drawer is needed. Alternatively, many restaurants draw expenses from the cash register. This is perfectly acceptable, just make sure to record the expense and file the invoice. Record final expenses and revenues separately at the end of the night.

Your bank will most likely be closed long before your restaurant closes, so it is best to take care of the nightly keep on the following business day. As you can imagine, you might be in the possession of a large amount of cash some Sunday night. For this reason, it is important to install a safe in your restaurant. This ensures that the staff do not have access to a large amount of cash towards the end of the weekend.

Luckily, most consumers pay with credit cards nowadays, limiting contact with cash. Before you open your restaurant, it is important to set up a merchant account with a credit card processor. Make sure to learn the rules of being a merchant, since processing mistakes can lead to lost revenue.

IDENTIFYING FIXED COSTS AND VARIABLE COSTS

As you open your restaurant, it is important to get an early sense of your fixed costs and variable costs. Fixed costs are costs you will incur every month, no matter how busy your restaurant is. Variable costs depend on how busy you are on a month-to-month basis. An example of a fixed cost includes your rent; and a variable cost is the cost of ingredients.

For fixed costs, you need to consider rent, water, electric, gas, permits, as well as full-time employee's wages. It is hard to reduce fixed costs, but there are a few steps you can take to reduce the financial burden. For instance, you can turn your gas off when a stove is not in use. By taking steps such as this, you can certainly see the savings over the course of a year.

In terms of variable costs, these costs are set by how busy you are. For instance, if you are a very busy restaurant, you will sell a lot more salad greens than a slow restaurant. For this reason, you can expect to spend a lot more on salad greens. Busy restaurants also have labour costs which can seem variable. For instance, if you are very busy on a Friday but dead on a Monday, your labour cost will seem more variable in nature. If this is the case, simply treat your labour cost as a variable cost. In time, you will learn to distinguish which costs vary and which costs remain constant. Record these costs and assign them a title of fixed or variable. Work on the variable costs and accept the fixed.

CONTRACTS

When signing contracts in a restaurant environment, it is important to proceed with caution. An offer from a linen company which seems like a great deal might turn out to be a nightmare six months down the line. Sometimes, a company will approach before the opening with a cash offer to allow their customers to redeem credit card points at your restaurant. While the cash injection might seem like a good idea, the discount offered to the guest might be so great, you end up losing a lot of money on the deal. With this sort of deal, you are unlikely to get out of the contract without some penalty. Before you open, you will need to sign contracts with the suppliers of goods, especially if you are offered credit terms. Make sure to have your legal adviser review your contracts if they seem confusing. Otherwise, it is a good idea to avoid signing contracts whenever possible.

You might be tempted to make your employee sign a contract. Within this sort of contract, you can limit liability, assert a confidentiality clause and list reasons for termination. To make this sort of agreement seem less to your staff, have your employee sign their employee manual. This will help to emphasize the importance of the workers contract.

FOOD SAFETY

To prepare and serve foods in a safe manner, it is important to follow the guidelines set in this chapter. Millions of people become sick each year and thousands die after eating contaminated or mishandled foods. Serving safe food has numerous benefits. By preventing food borne illness outbreaks, establishments can avoid legal fees, medical claims, wasted food, bad publicity and possibly, closure of the restaurant.

Most of the outbreaks of food borne illnesses are caused by food handling errors. It makes sense to implement the most effective food sanitation system possible. Careful food handling and sanitation practices can control the factors that can lead to food borne illnesses.

Hazards can be introduced into foodservice operations in numerous ways: by employees, food, equipment, cleaning supplies and customers. The hazards may be biological (including bacteria and other microorganisms), chemical (including cleaning agents) or physical (including glass chips and metal shavings).

Microbiological hazards (bacteria in particular) are considered the greatest risk to the food industry. Bacteria usually require food, acidity, temperature, time, oxygen and moisture in order to grow. Controlling any or all of these factors can help prevent bacterial growth.

There are a number of central themes when it comes to food borne illness. The most common themes can be describes as follows:

- ✓ Improper cooling of foods
- ✓ Advance preparation of food (with a 12-hour or more lapse before service).
- ✓ Infected employees who practice poor personal hygiene.
- ✓ Failure to reheat cooked foods to temperatures that kill bacteria.
- ✓ Improper hot holding temperatures.
- ✓ Adding raw, contaminated ingredients to food that receives no further cooking.
- ✓ Foods from unsafe sources.
- ✓ Cross contamination of cooked food by raw food, improperly cleaned and sanitized equipment, or employees who mishandle food.
- ✓ Improper use of leftovers.
- ✓ Failure to heat or cook food thoroughly.

The first line of defence when it comes to food safety can be traced to the receiving of the foods. All foods should be in excellent condition when they arrive. The quality and temperature of foods should be closely monitored at delivery. Check frozen foods for signs of thawing and refreezing, such as blood on meat boxes, fluid leakage, frozen liquids at the bottom of the food carton or large ice crystals in or on the product. Reject canned goods that are dented, bulging or rusty. Finally, refrigerate potentially hazardous foods immediately.

After monitoring receiving and storage for safety, it is essential to avoid cross-contamination and temperature/time abuse during preparation, cooking, serving and cooling. Calibrated thermometers should be used to monitor temperatures.

While cooking, make sure to avoid cross-contamination. This occurs when harmful bacteria are transferred from one food to another by means of a nonfood surface, such as utensils, equipment or human hands. Cross contamination can also occur food to food, such as when thawing meat drips onto ready-to-eat vegetables.

Since foods are often prepared (or cooked) well ahead of time, it is important to cool these foods quickly. To complete a proper system of cooling, label and date food before putting it into cold storage. Make sure to cool foods from 140 to 70°F within 2 hours and from 70 to 41°F within 4 hours. Do not cool food at room temperature before putting in the cooler. To assure your foods cool quickly, divide foods into smaller batches and put in shallow 4-inch deep metal pans. Set the open pans on the top shelf of the cooler and cover the food after it has cooled. Use an ice bath to speed cooling. Place a container of food into a larger container filled with ice water to reduce cooling time. Stir frequently during chilling to promote cooling and measure temperature periodically.

After cooling foods, you will eventually have to reheat those foods for service. With this said, it is important to heat these foods to a certain temperature and only hold these foods at the warm temperature for a specific amount of time. Reheat previously-prepared foods to at least 165°F for 15 seconds within 2 hours is recommended. Make sure to reheat leftover foods one time only. Finally, do not reheat foods in hot holding equipment such as steam tables.

Foodservice workers and home cooks must pay close attention to personal hygiene. For instance, workers who have a cold, the flu or another communicable illness, should not handle food. The following guidelines should be stressed to any worker dealing with food:

- ✓ Keep clean by bathing daily, using deodorant, and washing hair regularly.
- ✓ Keep hair under control by wearing a hair restraint.
- ✓ Wear clean clothing/uniform and/or apron.
- ✓ Avoid wearing jewellery, which can harbour bacteria and cause a physical hazard if parts fall into the food. Jewellery can also pose a personal safety hazard if it gets caught in the equipment.
- ✓ Keep fingernails clean, unpolished and trimmed short.
- ✓ Wear a bandage and plastic gloves if you have open cuts or sores. In some cases employees should perform other non-food-related tasks until the wound heals.
- ✓ Do not chew gum while working.
- ✓ Do not smoke cigarettes while performing any aspect of food preparation.
- ✓ Avoid unguarded coughing or sneezing. Wash hands after coughing or sneezing.

Hand washing is perhaps the greatest tool to reduce food borne illness. For this reason, make sure to always wash your hand before performing any task in the kitchen. In addition, you should always wash your hands after:

- ✓ coughing, sneezing, using a handkerchief or tissue.
- ✓ touching bare human body parts.
- ✓ eating, drinking or smoking.
- ✓ handling raw meats, poultry and fish.
- ✓ handling garbage, sweeping or picking up items from the floor.
- ✓ using cleaners and other chemicals.
- ✓ using the toilet.
- ✓ handling soiled equipment and utensils.
- ✓ switching between raw foods and ready-to-eat foods.

In addition to the above, you must always dry your hands thoroughly after washing them. Moisture or wetness transfers traces of contamination. For this reason, the last line of defence is to dry your hands. This is true for equipment and hands. Hand towels, particularly disposable paper towels, are greatly recommended.

Regularly touched surfaces also need to be regularly rinsed, for example, the water taps, where you turn them on with contaminated hands, and you wash, but then turn off the tap and carry on, so you will still lift off contamination from the tap which has not been rinsed.

How to Create Schedules, Rotas

Depending on the type of restaurant you decided to open, your staff schedules will vary greatly. Many quick service restaurants are staffed by students, so you are likely to have a schedule with many part time considerations in this type of establishment. In fine dining restaurants, the staff are full time professionals. For this reason, each member of the staff will spend many of their hours in the restaurant. Beyond the type of restaurant, the location of the restaurant will also place a crucial role in the type of schedule. For instance, in France, kitchen workers will work from 8am to 3pm then take a break. They return to work around 4pm and work until midnight. A very long working day, six days a week. In Russia, the kitchen workers prefer to work two days on, two days off. When creating your schedule, make sure to ask the staff what their preferred method of scheduling is. Not only will this keep the staff happy, it will allow you to find a greater number of workers when needed.

Unlike many other business models, scheduling for the restaurant is key to portraying the message of being organized, efficient and reliable; all of which are primary considerations for a diner. Being open means being ready for business in all aspects, from front to back office. There are services like lunch or meetings that are time sensitive so being open must mean a time you are open for business. On the other end being closed for business is not necessary the end of the work schedule. The kitchen may close but cleaning and putting away must form part of the closing down schedule.

The first task when creating a schedule is to determine the hours of your restaurant. If you open for breakfast, lunch and dinner, you will need a much larger staff compared to a 'dinner only' restaurant. Some restaurants are open six days a week while others open for the full seven days of the week. The extra day certainly requires a larger staff, since you cannot expect all your workers to come to work seven days a week. For this reason, you need to determine how many hours you can afford to stay open. As you first open your restaurant, it is always a good idea to open with dinner and lunch then work towards breakfast if profitable. There is no need to hire too large a staff for an unproven eating time.

Once you have determined the hours of operation, you will need to decide how many staff you need for each hour of the week. Create a diagram with seven columns, each representing a day of the week. Next, add columns to represent each position you need to fill. Determine how many hours you will need the employee to work, then use this number as a shift. With this said, you only need to figure out front of house hours. Kitchen hours run through the day. When completing your front of house schedule, make sure to have the maximum amount of employees during dinner and lunch hours. You can reduce the number of employees during midday in most restaurants.

For the kitchen schedule, most restaurants will have two crews; one working during the day and one working at night. The day crew gets to work before the restaurant opens to receive foods and prep. As lunch beings, the dinner crew arrives, and both crews serve lunch and prep for dinner. As dinner arrives, the day crew leaves. A very fluid arrangement. When it is time to create your kitchen schedule, ask your chef to draw the above-mentioned diagram. The chef will determine how many cooks will be needed and which hours they will be needed.

Kitchen Schedules

There are many types of kitchen schedules to choose from when opening a restaurant. Below, you will find a couple of sample kitchen schedules to give you a sense of how you should build your labour schedule. The same format can be used for the front of house.

KITCHEN SCHEDULE

DATE	7/12/2009 SUNDAY	7/13/2009 MONDAY	7/14/2009 TUESDAY	7/15/2009 WEDNESDAY	7/16/2009 THURSDAY	7/17/2009 FRIDAY	7/18/2009 SATURDAY
CHEF		ON	ON	ON	ON	ON	
SOUS CHEF	10 A - 6:30	10:30 A - 6:30 A	10:30 A - 6:30 P	10 A - 6:30 P	10:30 A - 6:30 P		
BAKER			7:30 A - 2 P	7:30 A - 2 P	7:30 A - 2 P	6:30 A - 4 P	6:30 A - 2 P
AM COOK	6:30 A - 11 A	6:30 A - 2 P	6:30 A - 2 P	6:30 A - 2 P	6:30 A - 2 P		
PM COOK	9:30 A - 6:30 P	9:30 A - 6:30 P			9:30 A - 6:30 P	9:30 A - 6:30 P	9 A - 6:30 P
PM COOK	7:30 A - 11 A	7:30 A - 11 A	10 A - 2 P			9:30 A - 6:30 P	9 A - 6:30 P
PREP COOK			3 P - 6:30 P	9:30 A - 6:30 P	10 A - 2 P	10 A - 5 P	7:30 A - 11 A
DISHWASHER	8 A - 2:30 P	8 A - 2:30 P	8 A - 2:30 P			7:30 A - 2:30 P	8 A - 2:30 P
DISHWASHER	5 P - 8 P			8 A - 2:30 P	8 A - 2:30 P		5 P - 8 P
DISHWASHER		5 P - 8 P	5 P - 8 P	5 P - 8 P	5 P - 8 P	5 P - 8 P	
DISHWASHER		5 P - 8 P	5 P - 8 P	5 P - 8 P	5 P - 8 P	5 P - 8 P	

ANY SHIFT 6 HOURS OR MORE REQUIRES 1/2 HOUR BREAK!

PLEASE CLOCK IN AND OUT ON THE CORRECT TIMES ACCORDING TO YOUR SCHEDULE!

SCHEDULE SUBJECT TO CHANGE AT ANY TIME WITHOUT NOTICE!

JOB POSITION	MON			TUES			WED			THURS			FRI			SAT			SUN		
	HRS	Cost ($)	HRS (#)	HRS	Cost ($)	HRS (#)	HRS	Cost ($)	HRS (#)	HRS	Cost ($)	HRS (#)	HRS	Cost ($)	HRS (#)	HRS	Cost ($)	HRS (#)	HRS	Cost ($)	HRS (#)
Server	9-5	17	8	9-5	17	8	9-5	17	8	9-5	17	8	9-5	17	8	9-5	17	8	9-5	17	8
Server	10-3	11	5	10-3	11	5	9-2	11	5	9-2	11	5	9-2	11	5	9-2	11	5	10-3	11	5
Server	10-3	11	5	10-3	11	5	10-3	11	5	10-3	11	5	10-3	11	5	10-3	11	5	10-3	11	5
Server	10-3	11	5	10-3	11	5	10-3	11	5	10-3	11	5	10-3	11	5	10-3	11	5	10-3	11	5
Server	11-8	19	9	11-8	19	9	10-3	11	5	10-3	19	5	10-3	11	5	10-3	11	5	11-8	19	9
Server				3-9	13	6	11-8	19	9	11-8	13	9	11-8	19	9	11-8	19	9	3-9	13	6
Server	4-10	13	6	4-10	13	6	3-9	13	6	3-9	13	6	3-9	13	6	3-9	13	6	4-10	13	6
Server	6-11	11	5	6-11	11	5	4-10	13	6	4-10	13	6	4-10	13	6	4-10	13	6	6-11	11	5
Server							6-11	11	5	6-11	11	5	4-11	15	7	4-11	15	7			
Server													6-11	11	5	6-11	11	5			
Grill	8-4	72	8	8-4	72	8	8-4	72	8	8-4	72	8	8-4	72	8	8-4	72	8	8-4	72	8
Fry	9-3	54	6	9-3	54	6	9-3	54	6	9-3	54	6	9-3	54	6	9-3	54	6	9-3	54	6
Grill	4-11	63	7	4-11	63	7	4-11	63	7	4-11	63	7	4-11	63	7	4-11	63	7	4-11	63	7
Fry	5-11	54	6	5-11	54	6	5-11	54	6	5-11	54	6	5-11	54	6	5-11	54	6	5-11	54	6
Dishes	8-4	48	8	8-4	48	8	8-4	48	8	8-4	48	8	8-4	48	8	8-4	48	8	8-4	48	8
Dishes	5-11	36	6	5-11	36	6	5-11	36	6	5-11	36	6	5-11	36	6	5-11	36	6	5-11	36	6
TOTALS:	MON	419	84	TUES	431	90	WED	442	95	THUR	457	95	FRI	457	102	SAT	457	102	SUN	431	90

Weekly Total: $3,079
Hours: 659

Front Office (Floor) and Upper Office (Admin) Schedules

The front of house schedule should be based on the type of restaurant you open. As mentioned, a quick service restaurant will be staffed by students and part-timers, so make sure to create more part time positions than full time positions for this type of restaurant. Front of house staffs tend to prefer part time schedules, so use this to your advantage. Only having to hire someone for three hours can save a lot of money in the long run, so offer part time options if possible. With this said, it is important to hire employees on the front of house staff who can commit a large amount of time to the restaurant. These employees tend to come to work once lunch starts and leave as soon as dinner begins to slow.

While everyone in the restaurant tends to work odd and long hours, the administrative staff does not have to. Instead, try and offer your administrative staff normal working hours, Monday to Friday, 9am to 5pm. There is no need to hire an accountant during the weekend, so keep this crew well organised during the day.

Staying Organised

Staying organised in the restaurant is crucial for so many reasons. Firstly, you need to maintain organised invoices and bills to accurately judge your profit margin. You need to keep an organised labour schedule to make sure shifts do not go unfilled. In order to maintain a highly organised restaurant, make sure to consider the four pillars of organisation: Supervision, Management, Responsibility and Liability.

To stay organised, you need to continuously supervise your restaurant. Every day, you should study the financials of the business. Look at invoices and expenses, gross revenues, frequency of an item being ordered, to name a few critical measures. Make sure the correct forms have been filled out by your staff and that the person organising the data has signed and dated the forms. Spend time in the restaurant not only eating dinner, but observing employees and how they interact with the guests. Spend a day in the kitchen to get to know the back of house staff, as well as learn what it takes to produce each recipe. Through supervision, you can get a firm sense of your business.

Management is the second key to restaurant organisation. You need to have competent managers in order to maintain the quality and profitability of your restaurant. Managers can foresee problems before they occur and observe problems in the making. Managers can quickly correct problems when an employee does not know the solution, so it is important to continuously communicate with your management. To assure yourself that your managers are performing their functions with a high degree of competence, perform a review every three to six months. Here, you will be able to judge the success of your management.

Responsibility is the third key to a highly organised restaurant. You need to instil a high degree of responsibility in your staff. If a waiter forgets a customer's drink, they should feel responsible for disappointing the customer as well as affecting the bottom line of the restaurant. If a cook overcooks a steak, they should feel responsible for wasting the cost of the steak. While you do not want to be critical of your workers all the time, you certainly want them to take responsibility for their mistakes.

Liability is the fourth most important aspect of staying organised in the restaurant. If you do not stay highly organised, you are prone to be open to certain liabilities. For instance, if the tax authority wants to perform an audit to make sure you have collected the correct amount of tax, having detailed records is crucial to avoid any tax liability. If a customer claims they have been poisoned by the mussels served in your restaurant, having the tags from the bag of mussels will go a long way towards limiting your liability. By thinking of your liabilities, you can decide which aspects of your business you need to record and keep organised.

How to Manage a Restaurant Worker

Restaurant workers can certainly be a different breed. The culture of the restaurant is not like your traditional office position, so you can expect a much more personal relationship with your staff. With this said, it is important to instil a sense of discipline and respect in your restaurant staff. Do not allow the bartenders to consume alcohol freely. Instead, allow the staff to taste drinks as need after hours, and limit free drinks to one per night. This will keep the staff happy and eliminate the chances of your staff becoming drunk or drinking away the profits.

With the kitchen staff, you can assume a worker or two will come to work with a hangover. Instead of being annoyed at their physical state, get annoyed if they perform underpar or show up late. The act of coming to work with a hangover in the restaurant is not a sin, but showing up late certainly is. When managing the kitchen worker in terms of technique, it is important to demonstrate to the cook how to create a dish, then allow them the freedom to prepare for service as needed. For instance, you should demonstrate how to prepare a sauce, but not dictate what order the cook prepares for service. While you need to maintain standards, make sure to give your cooks freedom in the kitchen. As highly skilled workers who repeat the same actions again and again, you will be surprised how a cook can make a recipe more efficient in time. In this way, let the cooks find the best ways to manage the kitchen.

In a restaurant, you do not want to micromanage each process. Instead, it is best to put systems in place and judge the results of the system. If your restaurant is not functioning at its highest level, then it is time to look into the micro-aspects of the operation. If you micromanage your restaurant all the time, the staff will develop a sense of low-morale. This should be avoided at all costs. Instead, make sure to solve problems with your staff, not against them.

It also important to remember that staff turnover in the restaurant industry is rather high. In fact, it's the highest of all industries. Part of it is the aspect of employing temporal or passing through workers, such as students. One of the key improvements aimed to address this is by continually motivating and managing staff well. We are in an era where an increasing number of people may be considering longer term specialty jobs in the industry, either for skills and career ambitions, or indeed for income. Management must then observe and encourage those that may see it suitable to climb the career ladder with the company and encourage them on. The more staff feels they are in the growth and expansion plans of the company in their own development, the more they will be self-motivated.

Compliance matters

Compliance is a critical step in the opening process. You need to make sure you obtain the correct permits in your local municipality. Permits can pertain to the occupancy of the site, health of the food and the ability to sell alcohol. For this reason, make sure to stop by the local council and ask which permits will be needed to run your desired restaurant concept.

Obtaining permits can be a process. Some localities require that you go through a number of inspections to obtain a permit. For instance, you might need an initial inspection to discuss your kitchen layout before you build the space, then an inspection afterwards in order to obtain the permit. To avoid any chance of confusion, make sure to constantly review your permitting requirements and important dates. Permits involving liquor can often be difficult to obtain. You might need to appear in front of a town board in order to receive the permit, and the space you choose might have a limitation in terms of hours you are allowed to serve alcohol. For this reason, you need to act on your liquor permit as soon as possible. Waiting to take care of the alcohol permit late in the opening process might mean you have a non-alcoholic opening.

Beyond the permits needed to open the restaurant, you will need to renew permits from time to time. For instance, the local health department might require that you file a yearly registration fee for your restaurant. Alternatively, your restaurant might be inspected every six months or so, and your permit might be withdrawn if you fail these inspections continuously. The liquor authority is prone to drop into your business from time to time, so it is important you keep a well-organized bar at all times. Remember, permits extend beyond the initial approval stage, and need to be considered throughout the life of your restaurant.

Music, Entertainment

Depending on the style of restaurant you want to open, you might be inclined to offer music or entertainment. For instance, live music on a Friday night can be a big draw, especially in locations which have a high degree of foot traffic. During normal nights and business hours, it might be better to offer a softer type of musical entertainment.

Here, the best option is to share music through the sound system. Choosing the correct music is critical to your restaurant. While we all have favourite musicians and songs, these songs might not be appropriate or well received by your dining audience. For this reason, it is a good idea to subscribe to a restaurant music channel. These channels are often run by people who specialize in creating music for restaurants, so you can be sure the selections will be appropriate for your restaurant.

Adding entertainment to your restaurant depends on the type of restaurant you open. For instance, if you open a fine dining restaurant, it is a good idea to leave the entertainment out of the equation. However, if you decide to open a family friendly restaurant, entertainment is a great way to keep families coming to your restaurant time and time again.

Section [5]
Building the Best Staff

The Key Positions of Restaurant Staff

The structure of your restaurant staff will vary depending on the type and style of restaurant you open. However, most sit-down restaurants tend to follow a standard staff structure. For this reason, we will discuss the positions found in a normal, sit-down restaurant.

Beyond the owners, the most important person in a restaurant, and the person with the most responsibility, is the General Manager. The general manager runs the day-to-day aspects of the business, interacts with customers, solicits the media, to name a few tasks. When hiring your initial staff, you want to first hire the general manager. Make sure to hire someone with a high degree of experience to assure your restaurant runs smoothly.

Beyond the general manager, other staff positions can be divided into two groups; Front of House and Back of House. The highest position in the Front of House is typically the Maître d'Hotel. In many restaurants, the Maitre D. and the General Manager are the same person, it is only in very large formal restaurants where these two positions are divided into individual staff. The Maitre D. is responsible for making sure the guests are happy with the dining experience, takes care of the VIPs as well as being assured that the front of house staff are performing their tasks with a high degree of integrity and formality.

The next highest position in the restaurants' Front of House staff is the Director of Beverages. The director of beverages is responsible for managing the bar and wine programs. For instance, the Director of Beverages will deal with supplier relations directly related to the drinks served at the restaurant. This might include dealing with wine companies, beer companies, soda suppliers and bar supply companies.

Under the Director of Beverages, most restaurants have a Sommelier and a Mixologist. A sommelier runs and directs the wine program of the restaurant. This position is a highly specialized position, so it is important to hire someone with a high degree of experience when it comes to buying and tasting wine. The sommelier will choose wines which complement the food served, so it is important to hire your sommelier early on in the opening process. The Mixologist is the person who runs the bar program at restaurants. They will be responsible for choosing the type of beers sold, as well as creating the cocktail menu for the restaurant. The position of mixologist is becoming increasingly popular in modern restaurants. The mixologist tends to manage the bar staff which includes bartenders and bar backs.

Beyond beverages, the Front of House staff will include a number of people to assist with service. The service is typically run by Captains, a group of waiters who are responsible for taking orders, describing the menu, interacting with the guests, among other tasks. Once the food is prepared in the kitchen, another member of the staff, the Runner, will bring the food to the table. Restaurants often have Servers who purpose is to remove plates from the table, replace napkins, refill water glasses, and other tasks, such as clearing the tables in between courses.

In terms of Back of House positions, the kitchen is run by the Executive Chef. Directly underneath the Executive Chef is the Pastry Chef and Chef de Cuisine. While the Executive Chef is responsible to running the entire kitchen, the Pastry Chef is responsible for running the pastry section of the kitchen. The Chef de Cuisine runs the remainder of the kitchen on a day-to-day basis. Below the Chef de Cuisine, most restaurants will have Sous Chefs. A Sous Chef manages the moment-to-moment tasks of the kitchen and assures the correct inventory has been ordered for each day of service. Beneath the Sous Chefs, each station of the kitchen is run by cooks known as Chef de Parties. This position is responsible to managing each station of the kitchen. For instance, most restaurants will have a Chef de Partie for the Cold Food, Fish Station, Meat Station and Vegetable Station. Below the Chef de Partie, the cooks of the restaurant can be found. Cooks are responsible for preparing the food for their particular station. Many kitchens also include cooks whose sole purpose is to prepare vegetables, meat or fish. Depending on the size of your operation, you may or may not need prep cooks. Finally, the last position in the kitchen, and certainly one of the most important positions in the restaurant, are the Kitchen Assistants, who load the dishwashers.

BUILDING A BETTER FRONT OF HOUSE STAFF

In order to succeed in the restaurant business, you need to make sure your front of house staff have tremendous customer service skills. No one likes to be served by rude staff members, and if you hire staff who do not have great people skills, you will quickly see your attendance numbers beginning to fall. For this reason, it is important to hire people with tremendous customer service skills. With this said, it is hard to determine how a staff member interacts with the guests each time they approach a table. While it is not appropriate or possible to audit every conversation, there are a few steps you can take to make sure you have hired the correct staff.

Firstly, to build a better front of house staff, make sure to hire a general manager with a lot of experience. Beyond experience, a General Manager needs a high degree of patience and hospitality. When interviewing the General Manager, make sure the person has a warm personality and smiles a lot. Try to stress the perspective employee, ask them a difficult question or two to judge their reaction. People who cannot gracefully answer such questions might not be a good fit for your restaurant.

The tone for the front of house is set by the General Manager, but it is important to hire staff who have a very similar demeanour to the general manager. Always make sure to call and check references to assure yourself that the perspective employee does not have a history of degrading fellow staff and customers.

While it is important to hire the correct staff to assure a quality dining service, the owners of the restaurant have a shared responsibility when it comes to building a better staff. For instance, if you pay your front of staff employees less than the average wage for your area and type of dining concept, do not expect to attract the best and brightest staff members in your area. However, if you gain a reputation for treating the staff fairly and paying them well, you are sure to hire the best staff possible.

Beyond manners and money, there are a number of strategies you can employ to build a better front of house staff. Try to hold regular meetings with the staff to address concerns, complexities and stories of interest. Sharing your thoughts with the staff, as well as learning from their input, will benefit your service greatly. Offering short courses to the staff, such as wine tastings and cheese education courses through local experts is a fantastic way to increase the knowledge of your restaurant staff. Another great way to keep a happy and reliable front of house staff is to offer financial bonuses based on performance. Through these methods, you are sure to create a front of house staff which is highly courteous and attentive.

BUILDING A BETTER KITCHEN STAFF

The kitchen staff do not interact with the customers, so the methods used to build a better system of working is quite different. Instead, the most important and challenging aspect of your kitchen relates to quality. It is very important to serve the same quality of food every time a dish leaves the kitchen. You can prepare a dish correctly nine times in a row, but if you serve a substandard meal to the customer on the tenth time, you might not see that loyal customer for a while. If a patron eats a bad meal at your restaurant, there is a very good chance they will share their negative experience with friends and social media. For this reason, it is exceptionally important to maintain a high quality of food throughout the life of your restaurant.

To start, it is important to remember your chef is the person who is responsible for the quality of the food. With this said, you need to make sure you give your chef the proper tools to maintain a high quality. If you plan on serving 500 dinners per night, and will only hire two cooks to assist your chef, you can hardly expect a high quality of food, no matter who the chef is. To maintain quality, you need to have equipment in good working order. For instance, if your grill does not heat correctly due to excessive grease, you cannot expect to produce a high quality steak from that grill. For this reason, it is important to make sure you give your kitchen crew reliable equipment to assure success.

In terms of the day-to-day ways to build a better kitchen crew, one of the most useful traits you can build in your kitchen is the universal cook. In other words, it's important to teach each member of the staff how to prepare each dish on the menu. This way, if a kitchen worker does not show for work or is sick, the quality of the food will not suffer. By teaching the entire kitchen crew each recipe, you can allow workers to change positions from time to time. Rotating kitchen positions tends to keep the staff happier in the long run. Beyond positions, it is important to give kitchen employees a break from time to time. Working in the kitchen can be physically difficult, so making sure to allow your cooks to rest from time to time will help when it comes to retaining employees over the long run.

How to Hire Staff

One of the hardest tasks to successfully navigate when opening a restaurant involves the hiring of staff. There are many places to search for employees, so it is important to invest your time and energy in the correct direction. Luckily, there are many online sources for finding employees. Beyond online, many regions and countries have employment agencies which offer a wide variety of staff potentials. Before deciding which direction you would like to go, create a budget in terms of advertising expenses and time.

In many countries, websites such as *Craigslist* are a great way to find employees. While there is typically a small cost to place ads, you are sure to receive many potential candidates from this sort of website. When hiring your initial crew of managers, make sure to place a different advertisement for each position. This will help to eliminate responses from people who are not qualified for the position. The better managers will only apply to positions which are job specific, so spending a few extra pounds on a number of specific ads. will help you in the long run. Once you have hired your initial staff, it is a good idea to ask them if they know of people who might be good employees fit for the new restaurant. Most managers prefer to bring an employee or two from their previous place of employment.

When hiring, each position should have a different interview focus. For managers, a large portion of the interview should include tasks which judge the financial understanding of the position. For instance, a general manager candidate should know the approximate costs of foods, beverages, utilities, and other expenses of the restaurant. Make sure to ask these questions during the interview. However, the most important interview you will conduct will be with the chef. The best way to hire a chef is to conduct the interview in two stages. The first stage should involve an in-person interview with a number of potential candidates. From this pool, pick three chefs or so who you think will be best for the position and ask them to cook for you. This is called a chefs tasting. Sometimes, you choose the ingredients and the chef will create the tasting from this mystery basket. Other times, restaurateurs prefer to let the chef be creative during the tasting phase. Either way, ask the chef to prepare three dishes or so. Carefully study the final dishes, weighing the positives and negatives of each chef. Using this method, you are sure to find a great chef.

While there are many more positions to interview for your restaurant, it is best to divide the process into two main categories, back of house hires and front of house hires. Make sure to involve the general manager during the front of house interviews. In fact, it is best to let the general manager organize the process. The same strategy works well for the chef. With years of experience, the chef will be able to determine which potential employees will work best for the concept and tone of the kitchen. With this said, it is important to review the CVs of each potential candidate with the general manager and chef to determine if a candidate is fit for the position, is being offered the correct salary, potential worries, etc.

The final aspect relating to hiring involves the 'When' part of the equation. You definitely want to hire the key managers of the restaurant well before the opening. However, you do not have to hire every member of the crew months before the opening. For instance, the first hire should be the general manager, who should come on board around two months before the opening. This will give you time to get to know the general manager as well as take care of tasks essential to permitting, hiring, contracts, etc. The next person to hire in the restaurant is the chef. You need to give the chef time to create the menu, provide tasting menus, find suppliers and so on, so it's important to hire the chef at least six weeks before the opening. If you can afford to hire the general manager and chef even earlier, it is always a good idea to do so. The next hires of your restaurant will be the sommelier, director of beverages and pastry chef. From here, you want to hire sous chefs and bartenders a week or two before the opening. Finally, you want to hire the complete staff three days or so before the opening. This will give the staff a chance to get to know each other as well as learn the menu. It is important to have a smooth opening, and hiring the staff a few days beforehand will go a long way in assuring a smooth opening.

EMPLOYEE INTRODUCTION AND TRAINING

Once you have hired the staff, it is time to introduce and train the staff in regards to the particulars of your restaurant. Before you allow the staff to interact with guests, it is important to teach them many aspects of the operation. Above this, you need to spend time reviewing the rules of your restaurant. Rules might include clocking in, payday, sick days, etc.

The best way to share the general rules of the restaurant is to construct an employee manual. This way, you are guaranteed to train all employees in the exact same way. Employees get a written copy of the rules, making it easy for them to follow the rules and refer to the book when needed. With this said, not all employees should be given the same employee manual. The rules of the kitchen are much different than the rules of the front of house, so make sure to organize the rules for each division of the restaurant.

Since you are opening a new restaurant, you will need to introduce every employee to the business. There will be many new faces, so there are a few ways to conquer this complex aspect of the opening. For one, make sure to set up a general meeting with all employees before the doors open. Ask each employee to introduce themselves to their co-workers. Beyond the introduction, try and have an informal tasting during the introduction. This allows each employee to taste each dish before discussing with the customers, and provides a valuable introduction to your concept. The best time to have this introduction party is three days or so before the opening.

Beyond the introduction, it is time to train the employees. As you know by now, the general manager and chef are responsible for the overall training of the staff. For this reason, it is important to allow your managers to set the training schedule as well as the main objectives of the training. Before the opening, ask both the GM. and the chef to write down all the important lessons they need to train the staff to do during the opening. As the months pass, the list of tasks will grow into a large document which can be used in the employee manual.

The front of house training and back of house training are very different endeavours. As you can imagine, the back of house requires more time to complete the proper training. Sauces need to be prepared, bones roasted, recipes followed. Depending on the size of your menu, it can take up to two weeks to correctly train the staff. With this said, it is important to organize the training correctly. The chef should take time to teach sous chefs and other kitchen managers each recipe. By teaching the managers each recipe, the managers can quickly teach the basic cooks how to construct each dish. As opening day approaches, the chef does not have to teach each employee each recipe. Using this method, the kitchen training process remains fluid.

When it comes to front of house training, the general manager can set the best program. The GM. should take time to review the CV of each employee and determine strengths and weaknesses. If you are opening a casual French restaurant and the staff consists of waiters with a background in fine dining, there will be little training to do. Instead, the training would only need to cover the restaurants protocols, the menu and wines. On the other hand, if your restaurant includes a wait-on staff with little formal training, you should plan on covering more basic issues such as how to serve the customers, how to use the Point of Sales system, to name two basic functions.

HEALTH AND SAFETY AT WORK

The most critical step of opening a restaurant is to assure the health and safety of your staff as well as the customers. As you can imagine, if a food borne illness outbreak is associated with your restaurant, you might as well close the doors. If an employee gets injured while at work, legal fees might force you to close the doors as well. Even successful restaurants fall prey to these mishaps, so it is important to spend a significant amount of time judging your liabilities.

This important aspect of restaurant management is now usually categorized into two distinct areas. First, the Health and Safety of the work environment, and secondly, the Health and Safety of the product - the food and drinks. Both must be upheld and would usually be brought to the attention of each and every employee before they start to work, as part of induction or initial training. It also needs to form part of the culture of the work place and company, to be in everyday awareness and compliance.

First and foremost, you need to construct a business which is free from illegal building procedures. For instance, make sure to use certified contractors, electricians and plumbers. This will help to limit any long term liabilities due to faulty construction practices. It is important to design your kitchen in a way which limits any chance of causing injury. For instance, do not place the fryer at the end of the cooking line. If someone losses their balance or slips on spilled grease, landing in the fryer, you might be liable for long term care. When it comes to flooring, make sure the proper tiles, carpets and mats are used in the kitchen. If an area of the floor is prone to flooding, you might consider adding a floor drain to eliminate the wet spot.

Beyond the safety of the kitchen, it is important to provide for the safety of your clients. For instance, if your dining room is rather dark and contains a set of stairs, it is important to illuminate each step so that customers can clearly see the obstacle. If a step is loose, make sure to quickly fix this problem before it has the opportunity to become a large problem. Courts tend to side with the customer, especially when it comes to restaurant injuries. For this reason, making sure the front of the house is safe will be critical.

The final aspect of health and safety which you must consider when opening a restaurant involves the safety of the food. To start, you need to purchase your goods from sources with a good reputation. Do not buy foods from people who drive to your back door with the deal of the year. These products are typically stolen or misrepresented. Beyond the source of foods, handling foods in your restaurant properly is important to assure the safety of your meals. Make sure your refrigerator is in good working order by placing a thermometer in each refrigerator and measuring the temperature every day. When preparing foods, do not leave them on the counter for more than the time required to make the recipe.

In general, the golden rule of food preparation is that a food will go bad in four hours. When making soups and stocks, it is important to cool them quickly in order to assure you do not hold a food above a critical temperature for more than four hours. Failure to follow this rule can quickly lead to a food borne illness in your restaurant. If enough customers get sick, an outbreak can occur, which can be picked up by the local media; a devastating experience for most restaurants. Finally, if a food goes beyond its expiration date, it is important to throw the food away. While this might impede on your food costing goals, the cost of using that expired food can be very high if someone gets sick.

Providing Customer Service

While the food is important, the way your staff presents itself to the customer remains the face of your brand. If you build a great marketing plan and menu, but your staff are rude, you are sure to lose a large segment of your potential market. Instead, it is important to build a clear sense of high customer service.

Customer service starts as you greet the guests at the door. Many restaurants hire a host or hostess to greet guests, take coats and sit tables. If this is the case, make sure your host has a very friendly appearance and is attentive to detail. Beyond the host, the waiters need to preserve a high degree of friendliness. The waiting-on staff need to keep a keen eye on each table, reacting quickly when a guest raises his or her hand for assistance. It is important to teach your staff that the customer is never wrong. If the guest says a cup is dirty, although the cup appears to not be dirty to you, it is always a good idea to apologize and provide another cup. In other words, do not fight the customer when it comes to the small details of the experience. Today, every customer can be a critic and a bad customer can often be the most vocal of critics, especially when it comes to social media.

As the owner, you need to have a solid sense of your staff's demeanour in front of guests, so be sure to take the time to address your customers directly. Once a dinner party nears the end of their meal, approach the table and ask them how the meal was. Ask about the service and friendliness of the staff. Another great option is to provide a customer satisfaction card with the bill. Here, guests can feel quite comfortable giving you their honest opinion of the meal. No matter which method you choose to judge your customers level of satisfaction, it is important to address any concerns they may have in an honest, unbiased fashion. If you get a reputation for having a high degree of customer satisfaction, success will come to your restaurant, especially in the long run.

Today, it is accepted that while the purchasing public are the primary customers (external customers), the secondary customers to the business (internal customers) are the staff , suppliers and every other person that has direct or indirect dealings with the company to contribute to the operation and processes. In this regard they also must be treated in the same manner and approach as external customers.

Employee Manual

The easiest way to train new staff in a restaurant is to create a clear and concise Employee Manual. Not only will an employee manual make the process easy for you in terms of time, you are guaranteed to train all employees in the exact same way. To make sure the manual is simple to understand and direct, it is best to create versions for the front of house and back of house. The overall manual may be elaborate but it must remain operational. A manual should be available for employees to view and review, but it is not practical to give a manual to every employee. Instead, summaries that will be at the fingertips of your employees for quick reference, especially in key areas that deal with the everyday operations, are the best way to drive home ways of working.

When creating the front of house and back of house manuals, both copies should have the exact same introduction. For instance, the human resource contact for your restaurant will be the same for the front and back of house, so you might as well make this contact section the exact same. Pay day will be the same, and the local requirements for informing employees will be the same. Beyond the formalities of employment, make sure to discuss the philosophy of the restaurant, how to file complaints, as well as incentives for great performance. With this said, it is important to discuss reasons for terminating employment as well as the disciplinary actions which might take place should a serious infraction occur.

When constructing the back of house manual, it is a good idea to introduce the chef as well as the style of the restaurant. Spend time discussing protocols for vacation days, sick days, clocking in, and so on. When constructing the front of house manual, the more general information you put in the manual, the better. For instance, you will want to discuss in detail the instructions for using the Point of Sales system. Make sure to discuss the rules of service: how to serve guests, the proper way to set the tables, etc., before discussing service tasks and after-service tasks. As you move beyond the opening, the rules of your operation might change from time to time. For this reason, it's a good idea to update your Employee Manuals from time to time.

Section [6]
Composing the Menu and Food Service Delivery

The Basics of Menu Science

Forming an enticing menu is not just the key to pleasing your audience, it is also the key in terms of profit. If your menu is not formatted properly, you might end up only selling items on the menu with a lower profit margin. Instead, you need to study your costs and profit margins, and emphasize items which maximize your profit margin. With this said, every type of restaurant requires a unique menu presentation. Formal French restaurants are divided into sections such as Fish, Meat, Soups, Salads and Starters. A quick service restaurant will have a much shorter menu and menu descriptions. Photos will be common on a quick service menu, but you will never see photos on the menu of a fine dining restaurant. For this reason, it is important to build a menu which strongly reflects your restaurant concepts.

To start the discussion of menu science, we turn to the casual, modern restaurant. Since this restaurant style is becoming very popular for its fair prices and pleasing ambiance, the casual yet modern restaurant tends to draw from both formal and quick service concepts. For instance, the items on the menu with the best profit margin tend to be isolated in boxes on the menu. For instance, the most profitable items, listed under a section entitled, *House Specials*, will sure to attract a higher purchase ratio. Another great technique to add to the meal total of a table is to make the starters section of the menu larger than the main course section. By bringing the eyes back to the appetizer section often, your customers are more likely to order a first course. Try adding beverages within this menu design as well. Instead of Coke or Pepsi, think beer and mixed drinks. By adding cocktails with a high profit margin, you will gain a powerful tool to increase your profit margin.

In terms of quick service, the simplicity of the menu is essential. Remember, the visuals, layout and pictures are essential to menu success. You do not want to confuse the consumer with too many options, which can often have the effect of turning people away from your restaurant. Instead, clearly label the name of each item. List the price of the dish, making sure not to use whole currency amounts such as £1. Instead, use £0.99 or £0.95 prices when listing partial pound amounts. People tend to be more accepting if the price of an item is £2.99 instead of £3. Another great tactic in constructing your quick service menu is to create off-menu items. Create a massive burger to sell to customers in the know, or sell a creative sandwich named after a local hero. While the average customer might not see the item on the menu, the secret nature of the menu item will surely be embraced by those in the know.

The fine dining menu is a very different science. Firstly, the items on the menu tend to be very descriptive in order to highlight the ingredients within the dish. Menus are written in a simple format which does not include boxes or drinks. Instead, a formal menu tends to broken into a few simple sections. Some fine dining restaurants choose to showcase their dishes by creating Starter, Main Course and Dessert sections of the menu. Secondly, many restaurants choose to add subsections to this format such as Fish, Meat, Vegetables, Soups, Salads, and so on. In order to highlight the more profitable dishes, try listing the most profitable dishes at the top of each category. The consumer tends to move their eyes towards the top of each category, so listing more profitable dishes here will certainly help in the long run.

Remember, the goal is to create a menu which is attractive to the consumer and helps to facilitate a greater profit margin. In order to maximize this relationship, you might consider hiring a professional to design your menu. Having a specialist take a look at your menu will pay for itself within weeks of opening. However, to give you a greater sense of your menu design, the following chapter discusses the basics of great menu science.

STARTERS AND BITES

Selling starters is one of the best ways to add to the price of each meal at your restaurant. In fact, if you can get your customer to order a starter, you can typically increase the price per guest by 25% to 50%. To this end, you will need to create a diverse set of starters. Make sure to include a few salads on the menu, especially since most consumers are looking for healthy dining options. Soups are a great addition to any menu, and it is important to add vegetarian dishes to the starters menu as well. Add a variety of fish and meat dishes. Serving a raw fish plate or sushi makes an attractive addition to many menus, but remember, you need to make sure the fish your serve on the raw plate is of very high quality and freshness. If you cannot guarantee these conditions, it's best to leave the raw fish off the menu.

A controversial component of starter items includes the selling of small portions of main course dishes. For instance, if a main course meal can be served in a smaller portion, many new restaurateurs might think it is a good idea to offer such an option. However, this can significantly lower the revenue of the restaurant. You want your customers to order an appetizer and main course, not two appetizers. To avoid this, it is best to keep the starters and main courses separate. However, there are a few cases in which main courses can be served as starters. Many starter menus contain a party platter which can be shared with the whole table. In this case, adding samples of a dinner menu can be a great idea.

Also remember not to confuse welcome bites with starter dishes. In some cuisines, the provision of the mains course may be perceived to be taking too long. Many customers tend to view this as inefficiency, especially when they feel very hungry. Offering them welcome bites usually portrays an element of a dining experience. It gets the customers to begin to appreciate you are serving them and sometimes this can increase the drinks orders overall orders, The offer of starters must still be made for the sake of upselling, but also will keep the customers dining.

THE MAIN MENU

When composing the main menu of your restaurant, there are a number of options to consider. Many restaurants like to serve a menu which is set and does not vary. Other restaurants prefer a format which allows the guests to pick and choose from the main menu as desired. The type and style of your restaurant will determine which main menu format works best for you.

For formal restaurants, the main menu can be either *a la carte* or set. A set menu in a formal restaurant is typically a three, five or seven course endeavour and does not allow for many substitutions. Beware, this type of menu can be tricky to serve. Many guests might be vegetarian, gluten sensitive, lactose intolerant, so you might find the set menu format a difficult sell. At the same time, if you hire a chef with an impressive background, a set menu might be a hit. The best way to approach the set menu is to offer two main menus at your restaurant. The first menu can be the set menu, while the a la carte menu serves as the second menu. If this is the case, it is also a good idea to include the set menu items in the a la carte menu. Many times, a customer will order a set menu item from the a la carte menu, then decide to come back to try the complete set menu item. This tactic can help to develop repeat customers. At the same time, if the entire menu can be found on the a la carte menu, you will have a hard time upselling the customer. For this reason, make sure to leave at least one item from the set menu off the a la carte menu.

Some restaurants serve a menu which allows the customer to choose a great variety of tastes. This is especially true in ethnic and tapas restaurants. For instance, the customer might order a standard protein and choose from a variety of vegetable and starch options. If this is the case, you need to make sure you offer a wide variety of options. Sometimes it pays to offer your sides with a set price for a number of sides. For instance, offer three sides for £5. Make sure to place the most profitable options at the top of the menu.

The way you set up your restaurant menu is highly dependent on the type of restaurant you open. If you open a fine dining restaurant, it is important to offer a set or a la carte menu. If you open a tapas or ethnic restaurant, you might want to create a menu which allows the customers to choose from a number of options and combinations. Make sure to study concepts which are similar to yours in order to find the correct balance when it comes to creating your main menu.

PORTION CONTROL

In order to successfully open a restaurant, you need to have a firm grasp on portion control. In many ways, the worst trait you can build into your restaurant is the leftover bag. Giving a leftover bag means you are serving too much food, and it also means you are giving away food for free. For this reason, it is important to build a strong sense of portion control.

When building the menu, the main course dishes should always be bigger than the starters when it comes to portion size. The one exception is the salad. With this said, you do not want to make the starter portions too large, since it might instil a sense of fullness in the guests. If this happens, they might not order a main course. A one dish meal reduces your revenue dramatically.

If you are opening a tapas restaurant, you want to limit the size of your dishes to four bites or so. Another tricky menu which requires portioning is the mix and match menu. Here, you need to make sure the sides you serve all have a similar value. For instance, consumers expect to see a lot of French fries on a plate, but do not typically expect the same number of asparagus on a side.

While portioning is an important customer related concept, it is also an important concept in terms of kitchen preparation. For instance, it is highly advisable to portion proteins before you prepare them. Cutting a steak before service to its desired size not only saves time, but allows the kitchen crew to correctly portion the meat. This will save money in the long run. In many ways, it is a good idea to portion as much of the prep. as you can in the kitchen, since this will help to gain a tremendous sense of mathematics in the kitchen. By knowing how many guests you expect for the night, the kitchen staff can get used to portioning and preparing a certain amount of food. The more organized you are in the kitchen when it comes to portioning, the greater ability you will have to reach your financial targets.

TABLE OFFERING AND PRESENTATION

When opening a restaurant, you might be tempted to add an interactive element to your table presentation. For instance, you might decide to buy a special trolley to display your artisan cheeses to the guests. With this format, you can spend time informing the guests of the particulars of your cheese selection. Perhaps the cheese comes from a local farm or has an interesting history. Restaurant guests love to be entertained, and a cheese trolley is a great way to entertain. By bringing the presentation to the guests, they are more likely to spend a bit more money to enjoy the added experience.

There are many other ways of presenting the food to the guests. For instance in France, the Duck Press is an example of a very formal presentation. When serving duck, the whole duck is displayed on a serving trolley. The duck is carved and placed on a heated pan to keep the meat warm. The duck breast is removed first followed by the duck legs. The remainder of the carcass is placed in a large press. Beneath the press, a prepared duck sauce is placed in a small sauce pan. The bones are pressed, and the renderings from the press drop directly into the sauce pot. With this method, the sauce tends to thicken to its proper consistency. Next, the waiter cuts the duck breast and places the meat on a plate along with the duck legs and vegetable garnish. The dish is topped with the sauce and served. An amazing dish and display of knife skills.

Choosing a very formal and elaborate table presentation should be considered very carefully before opening your restaurant. Not only will it take highly skilled staff, a very formal presentation takes time. In other words, you will have to hire additional staff if your menu contains a high degree of presentation.

DESSERTS

The dessert menu is one of the most important additions to your restaurant. By convincing your guests to purchase a dessert, you increase the cost per person, a trait which will certainly help the bottom line. Besides ordering a delectable dessert, the guest will most likely order a coffee or an after-dinner drink. While you can expect a normal profit margin with the dessert, you can expect a high profit margin for the coffee and liquor. A great combination.

Besides desserts, the dessert menu should include a selection of coffees, teas and after dinner cocktails. It is a good idea to include a few creative coffees as well, since this sort of after-dinner drink is highly prized by younger restaurant guests. In terms of alcoholic drinks, it is always a good idea to keep digestifs, such as Cognac and Calvados, on the menu. Creating a warm cocktail as an after-dinner drink tends to be an attractive addition to the menu as well, so make sure to remain creative with your dessert cocktails.

Another option you might want to consider when serving dessert is the dessert trolley. While rather rare today, the dessert trolley was a staple of most fine dining restaurants before the 1980s. When eating in classically-inspired French restaurants, you are likely to encounter this unique and visual display of pastry talent. A dessert trolley typically includes large pies, tarts, cakes, mousses, ice cream and other pastry specialties. With this arrangement, the guest can choose a number of desserts to try. To serve a high variety of desserts while maintaining a profit, offer three desserts for a set price. This type of service will make your dessert course stand out from the competition.

Another great way to build a popular dessert menu includes creating 'off the menu' items. Many pastry chefs are always experimenting and working towards the next great dessert. For this reason, it's always a good idea to ask your pastry chef to keep a few recipes close in order to offer 'off the menu' creations. This tends to keep the pastry chef happy and brings an element of surprise to the meal.

Money sense of the Menu

When designing menus, you need to keep money in mind. For instance, if you open a quick service restaurant but charge £100 per menu item, you are business is not likely to succeed. Instead, it is important that you get a sense of your customers' budgets before printing the menu. To accomplish this, make sure to study your competitors' prices. Find the most expensive items, the least expensive, as well as the average price. Then, when designing your menu, remember to maintain similar financials.

At a quick service restaurant, people are more attracted to items which sell in terms of £0.99. However, in formal restaurants, another pricing strategy is more often used. Formal restaurants tend to offer menu items in terms of full pound amounts. Guests are not terribly price sensitive, so the price of the dish is less important in a formal restaurant. With this said, you do not want to overprice a dish just because you are opening a fancy restaurant.

Most restaurants tend to list a menu in terms of price per dish. The least expensive dishes are placed at the top of each category, while the most expensive dishes can be found at the bottom of the category. It is important to avoid this common mistake. Instead, make sure to vary the pricing in your menu within a category. While you want to add less expensive dishes to each menu category such as fish and meat, it is always a good idea to add a high priced item. Remember, the customer wants to see variation while you want to see profit. A low priced item has the same profit potential as a high priced item, so a healthy mix of high priced and low priced dishes is a sign of a successful restaurant.

Bar and Beverage

For many modern restaurants, the popularity of mixed drinks and cocktails is becoming pronounced. For this reason, it is a good idea to create a compelling bar service. In order to share your creative drinks with the customers, you need to do a good job describing each drink to the customer. For instance, if you create 12 cocktails for your menu, you also need to create 12 in-depth descriptors for the menu. Using highly descriptive and compelling words can help to sell a drink as well.

Most restaurants have a large and comfortable bar to allow newly arrived guests to relax and wait for their table. For this reason, customers tend to spend a lot of time looking in the direction of the bar, so it's important to highlight your bar program if possible. For instance, fill the wall behind the bar with your cocktail specials and descriptors. Placing your beverage menu in this sort of open space will increase the chance of someone ordering a creative cocktail. Remember, the bar menu should extend beyond a written menu.

At the same time, it is important to write a comprehensive bar menu. Here, you want to list your specialty cocktails, wine selections, beer selections, types of liquors, sodas, teas and coffee. Sometimes, the restaurant might run out of a certain type of wine, or add a wine to the menu. As you can imagine, you do not want to print a new menu every time you decided to add or remove a wine. For this reason, you might consider serving a daily wine menu which lists the specials and deletions.

How to Price the Food and Booze

Pricing remains the most important tool in order to maintain the correct profit margin. In terms of quantity of business, the restaurant will most likely end up making half its money from the kitchen and half its money from the bar. As you can imagine, the profit margin for the booze is greater than the profit margin for the kitchen. However, the kitchen is typically the aspect of your restaurant which draws a crowd. For this reason, the relationship of the bar to kitchen is very important. To price your foods, the first place to turn should be your competition. Make sure to study their menus to determine what prices they charge for each item. Also pay attention to the portion size. Once you have this data, it is time study your own menu data.

To study your own menu data, you need to determine the cost for each recipe. Study your invoices and portion sizes to determine an educated guess in terms of the overall recipe cost. The cost of the recipe should be around 25% of the price of a dish, so simply multiply the cost by 4. For example, if it costs you £5 to create a dish, you should charge £20 for the dish. This makes sure you account for the cost of labour, gas, equipment, and so on. Next, compare this data to your competitors. If your costs and prices are higher, you might want to reduce the price of your dish or cut the size of the portion. In most restaurants, a few dishes will be offered which give the restaurant a smaller profit margin. These sorts of dishes are meant to bring customers into the restaurant as well as to highlight the specialty of the restaurant. For this reason, you might decide to increase the allowable cost for these dishes to attract more customers. A cost ratio of 50% instead of the traditional 25% is acceptable, provided it is managed with car. If the dish becomes too popular, it is perfectly acceptable to raise the price by 10% or 15% to account for the potential loss of profit.

Pricing the booze menu is the key to hitting the correct profit margin for the restaurant. In fact, most of your profit will come from the bar menu. As a standard profit margin, most restaurants charge 400% over the cost of the beverage. For instance, if the cost of a bottle of beer to you is £2, you should charge £8. The same profit margin for wine should be expected, while cocktails can create very high profit margins for the restaurant. With a carefully constructed cocktail, you can see a return of up to 1000%.

CROSS SELLING AND UPSELLING ON MENUS

Cross selling and upselling are the key to bringing in a higher profit margin. For instance, if a guest chooses a wonderful steak, you might decide to recommend a particular red wine to accompany the steak. If the steak is offered with a potato, you might decide to recommend a few toppings to round out the meal, at an additional charge of course. To make the meal even more delectable, you might decide to offer a lobster tail with the steak. If an Irish Coffee is chosen by the customer, perhaps adding an ounce or two of a white chocolate whipped cream might add to the beverage, at an additional price, of course. Cross selling can also be used for other services such as outside catering or a party within the restaurant. And indeed other market segments as the staff identify through the interaction with the guest. These are just a few ways to upsell in a restaurant.

Section [7]
The Pre-Opening

At this point in the book, you are well aware of the financials of opening a restaurant, hiring staff, building a successful concept, to name but a few of the topics discussed earlier. Now that you have built a solid and organized business plan, found your space and determined the best path of marketing, it is time to works towards the opening of your restaurant. In other words, it is time to take care of the Pre-Opening tasks.

There are a number of important tasks to complete before you open your restaurant. First, you need to decorate your restaurant, then purchase chairs, tables, lamps and other hardware. You need to make sure the kitchen has been correctly fitted out with the proper cooking equipment, and you need to purchase your Point of Sales system. It is a good idea to constantly check on the status of your permits and it is important to begin the process of navigating your first inventory ordering lists.

This chapter is meant to emphasize the complexities you might face during the pre-opening as well as help you organize the process in a clear and concise manner. Remember, each restaurant tends to have a unique set of pre-opening tasks to complete, so it is important to think of how your concept applies to the foundations discussed in this chapter.

DECO AND REFURBISHMENTS

Once you have found your restaurant space and signed the lease, the next step is to furbish the space as needed. Before you make major changes to the restaurant, it is best to consult the landlord and lease for allowable changes and construction. If you tear down a wall, for example, and then find out afterwards that the landlord does not allow it, you might be forced to delay your opening to fix the wall, although you will gain a greater understanding of the rules as assigned in your contract. To avoid this, make sure to discuss with the landlord, prior to signing the lease, what can be done in terms of construction and what cannot be done. Also make sure to discuss what repairs you will be required to pay for and what expenses the landlord will cover.

The first task when furbishing your restaurant is to judge what needs to be done. Make a list, and assign a level of complexity for each task. For instance, painting your restaurant will typically be considered a task of low complexity, while adding an extra bathroom would be considered a major construction.

Some restaurateurs decide to hire a contractor to manage the construction of their restaurant. While this option is more expensive than self-construction, a contractor will work within the local building codes which must be followed to open a restaurant. For this reason, you should always hire a contractor for major construction. Make sure the contractor remains on schedule during the construction phase, for delays can lead to additional costs as well as a delayed opening. To avoid delays, do not add to the construction plans or change your mind during the build.

During the construction stage, it is a good idea to start thinking about the water and electric needs of the space. For instance, make sure you have addressed all power needs for your operation, adding electric sockets where needed. Make sure the water lines and drainage line have been added to all sinks behind the kitchen. It is best to take care of these tasks well before the opening.

Now that you have completed the construction work of your restaurant space, it is time to furbish the walls and floors. For instance, you might decide to add mirrors, paintings, advertisements or pieces of flair to your walls. Lighting is another important task to manage during this phase. For the most professional look, consider hiring an interior designer.

Once the walls and décor have been completed, it is time to turn to the table and chairs for your restaurant. Placement and size of tables and chairs is a critical arrangement. If you do not put enough tables and chairs in your restaurant, you will not realise your potential profit. Too many table and chairs and guests will find your restaurant overcrowded and uncomfortable. For this reason, make sure to spend time walking around the dining room to gauge the relationship of comfort to profit. With this said, it is always easier to add furniture than it is to return it.

The style of chair is very important to the guest experience. For instance, if you are opening a quick service restaurant, the quality of the chair is less important. Plastic chairs tend to work well in quick service restaurants since they are easy to clean and cheap. There is no long term sitting requirement in a quick service restaurant, so the comfort level can be low. However, in fine dining restaurants, it is important to purchase high quality chairs. The guests will be sitting for up to three hours, so you want to make sure they can remain comfortable in their chairs for an extended period of time.

In quick service restaurants, the tables should be easy to clean and durable. Style is not terribly important, but you need to make sure the table stands up to abuse over the long run. A sign of worn down tables can turn customers away from your business, so a strong and proven material is a good investment. While quick service restaurants display the surface of their table, fine dining can be quite different. Most fine dining restaurants cover their tables with linens, so the appearance of the table itself is not very important. Instead, the table in a fine dining restaurant tends to be polished wood. If you are opening a fine dining restaurant, make sure to invest in high quality linens to cover your table.

Beyond tables and chairs, it is a good idea to consider the additional pieces of furniture you plan on adding to your restaurant. For instance, you may need to put a waiter's station in the dining room, so it is important to consider the space needed to hold this station, as well as the way the station might affect your dining table layout. A few more considerations include the placement of waste paper baskets and bins, and the placement of Point of Sales systems, entry ways and exits. Make sure to spend time thinking of each and every possibility when it comes to furbishing your space.

BUYING ESSENTIAL EQUIPMENT

During the opening process, one of the most expensive and important purchases you will make involves equipment. Most of the equipment you buy will be used in and by the kitchen. However, it is important to remember that you will most likely need to buy equipment for your bar as well. When buying equipment, you need to make sure you can fit the equipment in the proper place and you need to make sure you have purchased enough equipment to sustain your day to day business. To give you a sense of the types of equipment you might encounter in a restaurant, the following section details the requirements of a newly built kitchen.

Depending on the size of your restaurant, the first piece of equipment you are likely to buy is the walk-in refrigerator. A walk-in refrigerator requires a large, flat space in order to make sure your refrigerator does not tip in time. The area must be dry and not prone to flooding. The most important part of your walk-in is the compressor. The compressor is the cooling component of the walk-in. For this reason, the compressor tends to give off a lot of heat in the form of hot air. Many restaurants place the compressor on the outside of the building to eliminate this added heat. However, owning a restaurant in a city might limit your ability to place the compressor on the outside of the building. To deal with this dilemma, many people direct the heated exhaust from the compressor through a hose to the outside environment. This is highly recommended since it will greatly reduce the inside temperature of your refrigerator surroundings. On a final note, new walk-in refrigerators can cost a lot of money, so try to buy a used one if possible.

PERMITS AND LICENSES

During the construction and opening phase, you will most likely encounter a few permit requirements. Permits and licensing depends on the local environment, so it is important to contact your local council or government to determine which permits are relevant to your business. While most people understand the need for a health and safety permit, many people might not be aware of the lesser permit requirements. For instance, your local town or borough council might require you to gain a permit for rubbish collection. To make the permit process a bit easier to understand, the following section should be helpful.

The first permit you are likely to encounter when opening a restaurant involves the formation of the business. Whether you form an LLC or incorporate, the very action of starting a company in many ways is a permit. A formally organized business is permitted to conduct business within the bounds of the economy. For this reason, formally organizing your business is the first permit process you will encounter.

The next type of permit you should apply for involves the collection of taxes. In many areas, the local government allows the restaurant to collect taxes on their behalf. You should contact your local government tax department to decide which type of taxes you need to collect and how you remit this money to the government. While you will not have to collect money, and ultimately taxes, until you open your doors, it is a good idea to complete this task early in the process to eliminate required work as the opening nears.

Perhaps the most important permit you need to acquire when opening a restaurant involves the health and safety of your customers. Many localities will require you to get a certificate of occupancy, a process which covers the safety of the physical space. Contact your local council offices for detailed information on this process. Beyond the safety of the physical space, the most confusing and stressful permit you will need to get involves the local Department of Health. This permit allows you to legally sell foods to the public and typically requires an on-site inspection. Beyond the initial inspection, you will likely encounter unannounced inspections during the life of your restaurant.

There are many issues which you need to address to successfully pass your health inspection. For one, make sure to have the correct amount of refrigeration for your menu, since this tends to be one of the most important issues a health inspector will observe. It is a good idea to place a thermometer in each refrigerator to demonstrate your control of the temperatures of your foods. It is also important to complete your sanitation system before the inspector arrives, making sure to buy the necessary cleaning solutions, towels, mops and such. Make sure all your water lines are up to standard, paying particular attention to the drains of the kitchen. Kitchen drains often need to be built in a way which eliminates backflow. A failure to follow this standard will add weeks to your pre-opening plans.

Health inspectors want to make sure you are capable of eliminating food borne illnesses from propagating from your property. For this reason, they are highly trained to look for potential sources of outbreaks. To start, health inspectors need to make sure the employee hand washing stations have been properly marked and are equipped with filled soap dispensers, paper towels, a sink and a proper flow of water. They want to make sure you have the ability to clean silverware, glasses and plates. To cover this need, an industrial dishwasher is traditionally used in restaurants. These dishwashers are quick to clean the dishes (often less than one minute needed in a cycle) and can heat the water used to clean the dishes to the correct sanitary temperature. Beyond plates and cups, you need to have a system in place to wash the pots and pans. Most restaurants have a separate station for washing pots and pans, known as a pot washing station. The pot washing station will have a three bay sink in order to wash, rinse and sanitize the pots and pans as needed. Many times, the kitchen will use this sink for food preparation as well. For instance, a three bay sink is a great place to drain pasta. Just make sure to always clean the sink before using it for food preparation.

Often, the local health department will provide you with written guidelines in order to successfully pass your initial inspection. Make sure to follow this material with a high degree of care, for this is your best guide to correctly passing your local inspection practices.

The next permit you will need to acquire deals with the alcohol you serve at the restaurant. The liquor license is probably the most time consuming and stressful permit of a restaurants' opening. Beyond filling out an application and filing an application fee, you might be subject to additional review by the local council of your city. Beyond community boards and local councils, receiving a liquor license might require a background check of the owners. Sometimes, a restaurant will not open because one owner has a criminal past. For this reason, make sure to perform due diligence before choosing major owners of the restaurant. As soon as you acquire the restaurant space, be sure to start the liquor licensing process within days to make sure you receive the permit before the opening. This permit can take months to receive.

Depending on the local government, you might be responsible for acquiring more permits to run your restaurant. For instance, many local councils require you to obtain a permit for waste removal. Other localities will require permitting for the frontage of your restaurant. For these reasons, it is important to contact your local government to make sure you cover all the potential permits you need.

Point of Sales System (POS)

During the pre-opening process, it is a good idea to spend a lot of time looking into Point of Sales systems. A point of sales system is your way of creating receipts, informing the kitchen of orders as well as getting a sense of your financial numbers. Purchasing the correct POS system is important to your long term success, which is why we will spend a bit of time discussing the functions of a POS system in a restaurant.

To start, the waiters are the members of your staff who will use the POS system with the highest frequency in your restaurant. A waiter will take the drink and food orders from your guests and input this data into the POS system. The POS system will then send the relevant order to each station in your kitchen and bar. For instance, if a group of four guests order a pint of beer each, two steaks and two salmon dishes, the POS will send the beer order to the bar and the steak and salmon orders to the kitchen. The POS will also allow you to include placements of your guests as well as special notes to the kitchen.

Beyond sending orders to the bar, the POS will send the order to the kitchen. Many kitchens have multiple POS printers in the kitchen to share the order with different stations. For instance, the pastry station and savoury line will typically have their own POS printer. If a food prep area is in an isolated area of the kitchen, it is typically a good idea to add a POS printer. Most of the time, a POS printer will allow you to print on two pieces of paper. This allows you to create two tickets to share with the line. For instance, some kitchens will print two copies of a ticket and hand one to the hot line and one to the cold line. For four tickets, you just need to repeat the printing process twice, a task which is managed in your POS system preferences. When you contact POS providers, it is a good idea to describe your restaurant as well as your kitchen layout. This will help the POS company put together the most comprehensive system possible.

Beyond organizing and delegating orders, the POS system prints the receipts and bills you hand to your customers. Many POS systems include a credit card swiper to help with the billing process. It is always a good idea to purchase a manual method for writing invoices, order and recording credit card receipts just in case your POS goes down during a busy service.

Perhaps the greatest tools in your POS relate to the ways in which you can study the financials of your operation. By maintaining an organized POS, you can study the day to day financials, week to week, month to month, quarter to quarter or year to year. You can study the frequency in which each dish is sold, the most popular time an order is placed, even the popularity of a certain table can be extrapolated from this data. For this reason, make sure to integrate your POS into your accounting software. Spend time learning how to use each function of your program in order to get the most out of it. Your POS system can be a very persuasive tool in your restaurant.

CREDIT CARD PROCESSING

In the modern world, most of restaurant transactions are conducted through credit and debit cards. For this reason, it is extremely important to set up a merchant account with a credit/debit card processing company. When you swipe a credit card, the processor is the party which deals with bank transfers of the transaction, fraud and terminal issues. If you are having problems with your terminal or a certain transaction, the first person you should call is your card processing company.

Many companies will supply you with the processor for free. Instead, the processing companies make money by charging you a certain percent of each transaction. This amount is automatically deducted from the transaction balance of each day. Most credit card companies transfer the funds to your account within three days of the transaction. However, sometimes a credit card company will put a hold on your account if fraud is suspected or a customer disputes a charge. This can cause the company to freeze your account, which can create havoc with your business. For this reason, consider hiring two credit card processing companies. Once you are comfortable with the better company, close the other account. The best place to search for a credit card company to service your restaurant is your bank. Your bank will have an internal service or can recommend a company which works closely with your bank. This tends to reduce the amount of time you need to wait for payment transfers.

SMALLWARES

As the construction phase carries on, it is important to buy the smallwares for your kitchen. Smallwares refer to the pots, pans, whisks, spatulas as well as the hundreds of other required pieces of equipment. As you determine the style of restaurant as well as the menu you plan on serving, you can begin the process of putting this list together. To make sure you do not buy too many items or buy the wrong items, it is always a good idea to have the chef manage the smallwares process.

The best way to put together a comprehensive smallwares list involves the equipment book of your supplier. For instance, the company which sold you the major kitchen equipment will also sell smallwares. Instead of keeping every item in stock, many of these companies only receive the goods from factories when an order is placed. To give their customers a sense of what they can provide, these companies often have large catalogues for you to take home and review. As you turn from page to page, you will notice the pieces of equipment you need. Record what you need in a document and place on the side. Next, look through your recipes and kitchen layout to see if you are missing any pieces of equipment. Once you have studied each and every angle of the smallwares list, place the order. When placing the order, be sure to include the item name, item number and page number in the book. This will help to reduce any amount of confusion. By following this process, you will most likely have 99% of the pieces of equipment you need to open your restaurant.

GLASSWARE, DISHES AND SILVERWARE

One of the most time consuming components of the opening will be the time you spend buying glassware, dishes and silverware. While it might seem like a simple task, the sheer size and variety of potential solutions will take time to absorb. It is a good idea to plan on spending a good two days reflecting on the samples you see and feel.

Before you start looking at potential plates and such, make sure to do a thorough inventory in terms of needed items. For instance, if you have a restaurant with 75 seats, it's a good idea to order 100 plates of each type needed. While you might not use all the plates at once, remember that you will lose a plate or two from time-to-time due to wear and unexpected breaks. Sometimes, a line of plates or glasses will be discontinued. If you break too many plates and the supplier does not have any more, you might need to replace your entire inventory. Instead, it is a good idea to invest in extra plates. The same can be said for silverware and glasses.

A great way to eliminate potential plates, glasses and silverware is to consider your budget. Since you have calculated the number of plates, glasses and silverware needed, you can determine a per item price. By paying attention to this number, you can eliminate plates, glasses and silverware which are both above and below your budget.

It is important to buy plates, glasses and silverware which are durable and can withstand the chaotic environment of a professional kitchen. People will be able to recognise cheap plates, which can cheapen the perception of your restaurant. With this said, the most expensive plates (over £100 per plate) are the easiest ones to break. Your goal is the find a style and size of plate which balances quality and price. For this reason, it tends to take a lot of time to find the correct plates.

Once you choose the plates, glasses and silverware for your restaurant, it is a good idea to calculate the final cost. Many times, discounts are given if you buy a certain amount of plates, glasses and silverware. Discounts are typically larger for restaurants who buy their smallwares from the same company. Beyond discounts, ask yourself if you really need all the plates, glasses and silverware up front. Ask the supplier how common the plates are, and what wait times you might encounter if you needed extra plates, glasses and silverware sometime in the future. If you can eliminate 10% of your order, this can translate into thousands of pounds you can put towards your opening.

Initial Stocking

As the opening approaches, you will have completed the construction phase, decorated the restaurant, and purchased equipment such as plates, glasses and silverware. You have installed your Point of Sales system and you have received all your permits. Now, it is time to order your initial supplies.

When ordering your initial supplies, it is a good idea to start by ordering in terms of shelf life. Try and list your inventory lists in terms of dry goods and perishables then apply this specialized list to your initial ordering day. The first supplies you want to order involve the cleaning supplies. Paper napkins, plates, cups, soap, paper towels, toilet paper, bleach and ammonia, to name a few supplies. The supplies rarely ever have an expiration date, so you can easily store them weeks before the opening.

The next order of goods you need to order involve the dry goods of the restaurant. These food goods can last for weeks or months as well, but you definitely want to wait till after the construction of the kitchen and restaurant is complete before ordering any food goods. You also need to make sure that your kitchen smallwares have arrived for the restaurant before you order dry goods. If you order dry goods and do not have any containers to put the inventory in, you might have a difficult day! Dry goods include flour, sugar, coffee, ketchup, canned goods, salt, pepper, spices, pasta and such. For the first month of the opening, you do not want to spend a lot of time chasing down small, inexpensive dry goods, so make sure to order a large supply of guest sugar packets, straws, etc., in order to assure you do not run out of crucial supplies. With the million tasks to complete when you open, having a deep supply of dry goods will help tremendously.

Once you obtain the liquor license, you can begin to bring your booze to the restaurant. Call your liquor suppliers and have them make their deliveries. Once again, you want to make sure your construction phase is finished by this point; it is important to limit access to the alcohol when it arrives at the restaurant.

Now that you have your cleaning supplies, alcohol and dry goods, it is time to turn to your perishable goods. Perishable goods are foods with a rather rapid expiration date. For instance, lettuce and fish are two examples of perishable goods. Since they spoil quickly, you want to order these goods the day before you open the restaurant. With this said, your chef might want to prepare a few things a week before the opening of the restaurant. For instance, if you open a fine dining restaurant, your chef will most likely serve meat sauces which are a four day reduction. Because of this, you might need to order bones, onion, celery and carrot a week before the opening. To account for items which take days to create, ask the chef to manage the intake of perishable goods.

The day of the opening is the day you want to receive highly perishable items. For instance, it is a good idea to order the fish and herbs on the first day you are open. Make sure to keep the foods fresh by not getting too far ahead when it comes to ordering your initial inventory.

CALLING IN THE COMPLIANCE INSPECTORS

As you finalize the pre-opening tasks, your restaurant will be ready to open. Now it's time to finalize the process by calling in the compliance inspectors. Many inspectors will want to see your restaurant as it will be presented to your guests. This includes supplies and food. In fact, many inspectors decided to hold off on a passing grade until the restaurant is 100% ready to be opened.

Back when you first applied for your health permit, you were given forms to fill out and instructions to follow. Within this material, you will find instructions of when to contact the inspectors to come see your finished facility. When you choose your opening date, make sure to remember which day you need to contact the inspectors.

In the hours before the inspector arrives, make sure to go through your health and safety checklist. Make sure the bathrooms have waste baskets, soap, toilet paper and towels. Make sure each refrigerator is working and the thermometers work correctly. Finally, it is important to remove any remaining construction materials before the inspection. Clean all surfaces to remove any dust which might have settled during construction. When you are ready for your final inspection, you are ready to open your doors.

PUTTING TOGETHER AN OPENING TEAM

By this point in the process of the opening, you have most likely hired for the major positions of your restaurant. For instance, you have hired the Chef, Maître D., Sous chefs, Sommeliers, Mixologist and Waiters. There are a few final tasks to complete before you put this team to work.

The final employees you hire should start a day before you open. For instance, you can hire your kitchen assistants and cleaners a day or two before the opening. These positions require little skill, so the learning process can be completed on the go. By waiting until you are near the opening, you can save thousands of pounds in labour, which is money well saved during an opening.

Once the entire team has been hired, it is time to form the team into a successful group. Before the opening, try and bring all the employees together to mingle and introduce themselves to each other. Try to add a team building exercise to the meeting. A team which gets along is a successful team!

Choosing an Opening Date

One of the most unpredictable tasks you have to master during the pre-opening involves picking the opening date. It is important to choose an opening date early in the process to organize your marketing strategy and advertising campaigns. It is very difficult to correctly guess your opening date, especially when you are dealing with construction and supply issues. For this reason, you will need to hold off on choosing an opening date until the correct time.

The correct time to declare your opening date is about two weeks before you open. This gives you enough time to contact the health inspector to plan an inspection date. Two weeks will give you enough time to order supplies, hire staff and train them as needed. To make this process easier, it is important to have your marketing and advertising plan mapped out before you pull the trigger.

Two weeks might not be enough time to record and produce a radio commercial, but two weeks is enough time to submit your commercial to be run during the opening. You might not be able to produce a video in two weeks, but you can certainly create a pre-opening visual of your restaurant. Two weeks is enough time for newspapers to run your ads, just make sure you have finished the content of the advertisement before the two week mark. Finally, as the day of the opening nears, you can implement your online marketing scheme.

Social Media Integration

Before you open, you need to spend a lot of time working on your social media integration and outreach. Social media is perhaps the most powerful form of marketing today, so creating a well thought-out marketing plan can significantly increase your restaurants reach. Social media also tends to be cheaper than print media, although it requires a clever approach.

Earlier, you spent time putting together your brand, concept and initial marketing plan. As you approach the opening, you can add to your materials greatly. For instance, your restaurant is now finished, so you can create photos of your space. The silverware, glasses and plates have arrived and you have finalized the menu. With these materials, you can create attractive photos to add to your website and social media accounts.

Weeks before the restaurant is due to open, it is a good idea to start building your social media reach. Start accounts for Facebook, Twitter, and Instagram, as well as any additional sites you feel will work well for your business. Ask your friends to register a 'like' on your new restaurant page and offer them a discount for coming to your restaurant. Start following people on twitter who live in your local area to target customers. Post pleasing photos to Instagram of your space and food. Beyond this, you want to build a long term audience. Offer specials whenever possible, and make sure to advertise special meals and events.

While social media can be a powerful tool, make sure to not overdue your posts. Instead of focusing on the quantity of posts, make sure to focus on quality. You want your audience to be interested in all posts, emails and messages you send, so make sure you are focused on long term success. Blasting social media sites with too many posts can reduce their willingness to come to your restaurant.

Public Relations

In order to reach print, television and online media such as newspapers and foodie blogs, you might consider hiring a publicist. A publicist will act as your liaison between the restaurant and press. Publicists can be quite expensive but also a successful source of business in the long run. A publicist can easily get your restaurant featured in local newspapers and television channels, so hiring a publicist can be a great addition to your team.

Beyond contacting the media, a publicist can be quite helpful when it comes to putting together your marketing strategy. Having a high degree of experience, a publicist will know which concepts and marketing strategies have proven successful in your local area. They can help you to fine-tune the opening process, as well as make sure your restaurant remains popular and relevant for years to come. Before you hire a publicist, it is important to judge the previous work of the publicist. Are the restaurants they have worked with successful and well known? Are the restaurants still open? Consider the previous work experience of the publicist. A publicist with a lot of media experience will certainly have a lot of contacts in the business, a relationship which helps your chances of picking up lots of press.

Many restaurants who hire a publicist do so on a long term basis. In other words, a restaurant will hire a publicist for the entire life of the restaurant. However, not all restaurants need a long term publicist or have the budget for long term assistance. Make sure to discuss long term and short term needs when you first meet with the publicist.

Section [8]
The Opening

Congratulations! You have made it to the opening. So far you have accomplished a tremendous amount of work. You have learned the ins and outs of running a restaurant and executed the opening. You have finally arrived at the opening day of your business.

The opening of the restaurant can be a stressful or exciting process. If you have followed the steps listed in this book so far, your experience will most likely be stress free. Remember, the key to a smooth opening is organization. It is important to constantly organize and reorganize yourself. By remembering this simple rule, the opening will be a smooth process.

Now that you are ready to open the doors, there are a few important tasks to complete in order to steer your business in the correct direction. During the opening, you are sure to run into a few kinks along the way, so finding these errors and offering a solution is very important. On day one, you will most likely experience the most errors. In three months, you should have found all the errors and provided solutions. This chapter will help you during the critical stage of your business.

THE FRIENDS/FAMILY TEST RUN

Before you open your doors to the public, it is a good idea to celebrate your accomplishment by inviting family and friends to dinner. Being the first meal you serve, the formality should always be low and mistakes should be forgiven quickly. This opening night allows the kitchen crew and front of house staff to become comfortable with the restaurant and procedures. The staff will observe obstacles and find solutions to these obstacles. There are many benefits to the family and friend test run.

When serving a family and friend test run, it is customary to not charge your guests. Instead, you should invite your guests to enjoy the restaurant and menu without having high expectations. Besides, if you invite 75 people to your test run, you will have 75 people talking about your restaurant before it opens, which is a great addition to your early marketing plan.

To reduce the cost of your test run, consider serving a set menu along with some of the cheaper wines offered at the restaurant. Having a set menu will reduce the overall cost of the test run and give the staff a night where the learning curve is more manageable. Make sure to ask your guests what they think of the food and service. If their suggestions are good, try and implement them into your procedures and recipes.

The test run involving your family and friends should happen the night before you open the doors. This will allow you to minimize the expenses related to the party, but it will also reduce food waste. At the end of the party, discuss with the staff the complexities of the night. Listen to their suggestions and implement plans which are useful and solve problems. If the problems involve the POS or other documented aspects of your restaurant, it is important to update all relevant files and software if needed. By the end of the night, you will be ready to open the doors with a high degree of preparedness.

Marketing Your Opening

Opening day can be a tricky day to draw a crowd. Most people like to wait a few weeks in order to give a restaurant time to settle into the space. While it is nice to know these people will eventually come to your restaurant, the prospect of having an empty restaurant on opening night can be frightening. For this reason, you want to cast a wide net to fill your restaurant in the first few weeks.

For opening night, you might consider offering a free drink or a deep discount to customers. These marketing tactics will help to fill the seats as you open the doors. Make sure to highlight the exciting parts of your restaurant when conducting your marketing opening. For instance, if you have a beautiful patio bar located in a business district, you opening should include an 'after work special' or two. On opening night, you want to draw crowds which interact closely with your neighbourhood. For instance, if a resident or business loves your restaurant on the first day, there is a good chance you will see them come back in the following days.

Some restaurants open with grand displays and heavy advertising. Certainly, if you open a quick service restaurant, this tactic might help to solidify a busy opening. For quick service opening, radio and television tends to be a great place to draw in the local crowd. Having a celebrity appear at your opening can be a great trick to bring crowds, especially if your audience includes younger generations. While you have spent a great deal of time designing the façade of your business, you might consider adding a large amount of temporary marketing materials to the outside of your business during the opening. Signs and large banners can be a great way to introduce yourself to the neighbourhood.

When opening the doors of your restaurant, you are likely to encounter the largest marketing and advertising costs of your business. While you need to spend a lot of money to initially market your restaurant, it is important to remember that this cost will diminish in time. The quicker you build a loyal clientele, the quicker you can reduce the amount of money you spend on marketing and advertising. Reputations are the best marketing material any restaurant can have.

Soft Opening/Grand Opening

Depending on the type of restaurant you open, you might decide to have a soft or hard opening. A hard opening is also known as a grand opening. For most quick service restaurants, a grand opening is the only opening of the business. You need to have your procedures and recipes perfected before you open, so you might as well tell the world from day one. However, many fine dining restaurants do not advertise their opening for a couple weeks. This allows the restaurant to completely troubleshoot the bugs of their restaurant.

Soft openings generally occur in fine dining restaurants as well as casual restaurants. Here, the initial opening is not advertised, giving the locals time to stop by, as well as giving you time to perfect your restaurant. Reporters will have time to stop by to try your dishes and observe your ambiance. You will have time to judge the staff and make adjustments as needed. Then, after two weeks have passed, the formal opening, or grand opening, is announced to the world. By this point, the employees will be comfortable with their role in your restaurant, making sure they do not make embarrassing mistakes in front of paying guests.

Many times, a grand opening serves as a great way to bring a second wave of opening business to your restaurant. For instance, a quick service restaurant on a high traffic street will greatly benefit from day one. People will be curious about the new shop, and are more likely to choose your business over a neighbouring competitor. After the opening, you might see the amount of business fade a bit. Adding grand opening signage to your restaurant will certainly bring additional business. For this reason, you might consider two openings for marketing purposes.

OPENING DAY

Opening day will be busy no matter how organized you are, and you are unlikely to get a lot of sleep the night before you open the doors. You will be working very long hours and you will have to interact with guests from the perspective of a restaurant owner. The best advice I can give is to enjoy the day and take things as they come.

Depending on the opening time of your restaurant, you will need to arrive early. If your restaurant opens at 8am, it is a good idea to get to the restaurant at least two hours earlier. With the extra time, complete a final review of all your procedures. Test all of the essential equipment, making sure all of the key staff members are ready for the day, and the supplies are completely stocked. If you are organized early, open the doors fifteen minutes before 8am. Sometimes it's nice to know you are ahead of schedule. If your restaurant opens at six in the evening, try to get to the restaurant at noon. This will give you time to call people during business hours, receive orders and review procedures. If you are open from 8am to midnight, it will be difficult for you to spend the entire 16 hours on your feet. For this reason, you might want to schedule an hour or two break in the afternoon. Remember to manage your own working hours with the working hours of the restaurant. As you settle into the business, you can start to sleep more as needed.

As your first guests arrive, make sure to not smother them or stare. Since this is your first customer, your energy and excitement will be quite high. Do your best to avoid being overly reactive, since this might annoy your first guests. Instead, give them the normal amount of service and attention, and mention to them at the end of the meal that they are table number one. Make sure to keep the first bill you make!

As the diners enjoy your restaurant throughout the day, it is important to observe your staff and make adjustments as necessary. For instance, perhaps a server has not learned to correctly open a bottle of wine. If this occurs, take the server to the side and demonstrate the correct technique. Sometimes, a waiter will have trouble with the Point of Sales system. Since you have taken the entire course in regards to the software, take the time to correct the problem, making sure to explain what went wrong.

During day one, you might encounter a problem which deals with documentation, for example, a recipe might be too spicy and needs to be adjusted. Make the correction to the recipe book immediately so that the same mistake does not happen again. Often with a new POS system, your prices will change during the opening. For instance, you might have originally chosen to sell a bottle of wine for £45, but decided to increase the price to £50. You made the change in your POS system, but the price changes for some reason. Solve this problem immediately. Not only because you are losing money, but also because you need to get into the habit of solving problems as soon as they occur.

Not all your opening tasks relate to the front of house. Instead, it is a good idea to spend a bit of time in the kitchen to observe the procedures and flow of a dinner service. This can be a very fun experience, especially if you do not have a lot of experience in the restaurant business. Make sure to get to know the kitchen staff and ask questions about the recipes. If the service becomes very busy, it might be a good idea to leave the kitchen and stay out of the way.

As you make your way through the first day of business, you might be tempted to have a few drinks and mingle with the crowd. It is never a good idea to drink during the day, even if you are the owner, so make sure to save your own relaxation time for the end of the night. Besides, you need to study the financials of the day. This will be the first day you record your data and it will be the first day you use your POS software. Spend the end of the evening getting to know your software. How many salads were ordered? What was the average price per person? What was the total revenue? What percentage of sales came from food and what percentage from booze? These are just a few questions you should ask yourself at the end of the night.

Finally, you reach the end of the night. Now, it is time to spend time contemplating the day. You have worked hard to get to this point, so make sure you continue to work hard. Spend a few hours thinking of specific events, interesting financials and future concepts you would like to implement into your business.

WEEK ONE

As the end of week one approaches, you will be quite familiar with your staff and you will have worked out most of the kinks in your operation. You have served a lot of guests and you have observed a lot of great financial insight through your point of sales system. With this said, there are a number of events you might encounter during week one which are worthy of discussion.

First, it is a good idea to remember you might face an inspection during the first week which is outside the bounds of the health department. The local tax collector or liquor authority might stop by, so you need to be conscious of this possibility. A member of the press might stop by incognito to get a sense of your restaurant, so treat every guest as if they were a big time food reviewer.

You are likely to receive food orders during the course of the week. Fish typically arrives on a daily basis, while you will have received goods from the meat company two or three times. You will have received a produce order every day, linen orders, dry goods, and so on. In a few days, you can have a staggering number of invoices. It is important to keep these invoices and prepare to send payments to the suppliers. Building a system of organization for so many invoices is important in the first week. If you neglect this aspect of your day-to-day responsibilities, you will not be able to fix the problem months or years down the line.

As with statistics, the larger the sample the better the information you can extract from the data. For instance, after you serve 10 guests, you can gain some insights into their level of satisfaction, but you cannot say with a high degree of confidence if this data reflects the public at large. Instead, you need a large data set. Hundreds of customers helps, and thousands of customers give you a clearer sense of your business. Once you complete your first week, you will have a large amount of data, and a clearer sense of your business model will begin to develop. You will have the expenses for the week and you will have gross revenue. You can start to get a picture of your first week of profit/loss, but you can also get a sense of what dishes are popular. You can study the profit margins of the popular dishes and exploit this function as needed. For this reason, make sure to study your data in great depth during the first week.

By the end of week one, you should have solved 99% percent of the problems related to the kitchen and service. Make sure that the entire staff realises the adjustment to the business model, making modifications to document and charts as needed. By solving problems rapidly, you will quickly achieve a transition to a well-oiled machine.

Month One

As month one nears an end, your data set has increased greatly and you have solved nearly every problem you might encounter. By month one, you are sure to have lost an employee or two, and the stars of the staff are starting to demonstrate leadership qualities. While you might not be turning a profit at the one month mark, it is important to study your financials in detail.

The best way to study your financials is to compare them to your business plan. Study the business plan and determine which goals have been met and which goals still need work. Report on how your opening cost estimates compared to the actual costs of the opening and month one. Compile your data into a report and share this information with your investors. It is a good idea to demonstrate to your investors that you are operating your restaurant according to schedule and within budget. By offering a detailed review after month one, you are demonstrating your ability to run the business. In many ways, this quality is more important at the one month mark than the profit/loss statement.

At the end of the first month, it is a good idea to review your marketing strategy. Ask yourself which strategy worked best and pour your budget and resources into this channel. For instance, if you are getting a lot of walk-in customers through your fliers handed out on a busy street, increase this marketing strategy. While some strategies might be successful, others might not produce a tremendous result. It might be a good idea to put these strategies to the side until you can address them in a more suitable manner. For instance, if your television spots are not producing results, you might decide to save this expensive marketing method for another day. Perhaps you need to give an audience time to hear of your business, and then be invited to visit your business when they are introduced to your commercials in the future.

Many restaurants plan on opening for lunch and dinner, but only open for dinner during the first month in order to reduce the cash spent during the initial opening, as well as giving the staff time to get used to the restaurant. This is a great way to save money and maintain a high quality restaurant, especially in fine dining restaurants. If you plan on expanding your operating hours after the first month, remember that you will need to hire extra staff beforehand. Luckily, you will already have a number of competent, highly trained employees to help teach the newly hired. This is augmented if you created an employee manual. You do not have to place all the new staff in the new business hours. Instead, you can move some employees from the night shift to day shift. This will help to maintain the same level of quality in both the back and front of house.

The first month of business will be full of long hours and stressful moments. For this reason, it's a good idea to take a break towards the end of the first month. Make sure to catch up on lost sleep and take a mini-holiday if needed. You need to maintain long term health and strength in this business, so it is important to balance the long hours of the restaurant with your own ability to withstand the work. If you do not micromanage your restaurant, you will find it easy to take a few days away from the restaurant after a month has passed. As you complete the first month, you can start to set your sail towards completing the first quarter of business.

Month Three

The three month mark after opening your restaurant represents the first quarter of business. By this time you will have built a loyal clientele and continue to attract new guests to your restaurant. The weekends tend to be very busy, while Tuesdays can seem a bit slow. You have adjusted your level of staff to account for this trend. As you move towards day 100 of the business, you will have a great sense of your actual business model as well as the probability of running a successful business in the long run.

The note above which makes mention of the slow Tuesday trend is important to pay attention to. It is imperative to understand the most common days and hours that your restaurant is busy. By doing so, you can OPTIMIZE your labour schedule by reducing staff on the slow days and increasing staff on the busy days. For instance, many kitchens set their off days for Sunday, Monday and Tuesday in order to reduce the labour cost of these slow days. As the weekend draws near, you will need more labour to produce your food in a timely manner. Luckily, you have optimized your labour schedule to reflect this need.

Beyond the labour schedule, a number of important trends have formed in your restaurant. For instance, you are sure to have a couple dishes which clearly outsell other items of the menu. These dishes might be mentioned by the press in local newspapers and media as standouts, and your customers are quite happy with the tastes of the select dishes as well. Because of their popularity, these should be considered your signature dishes. As you change your menu in the future, you do not want leave signature items off the menu.

For the first month or two of your restaurant operation, you might not make a profit. Your volumes will still be low and your staff will need time to reach the correct level of efficiency. Mistakes might be made in the kitchen which eats deeply into your potential profit margin. For instance, if a steak is horribly overcooked, you cannot sell it to a customer. Instead, it is best to take the financial hit and hope to keep the customer satisfied. By month three, you should be able to get a clear picture of your profit/loss potential. Study your financials and determine which menu items have been successful and which ones are not. Study the profit margin for each. After three months, you might decide to eliminate a recipe or wine. This is especially true if the profit margin is low and the recipe requires a nightly preparation. At month three, it is time to make financial sense of your restaurant.

How to Remain 'New' Beyond the Opening

As a restaurant passes its opening quarter, the restaurant will still seem new to your local audience. With this said, it is important to keep in mind your operation is becoming older and less relevant in terms of the local, everyday conversation. To constantly bring in new business, it is important to remain fresh in the consumers' minds. For instance, you might decide to change the menu seasonally in order to share the fresh update with your current and potential customers. This gives you the opportunity to reach new clients and customers you have already served. If a customer enjoyed your restaurant the first time around, they are very likely to come and try your new menu, especially if you market the new menu in a compelling way.

Keeping your restaurant new requires tactics outside the bounds of a new menu. If you offer music or entertainment during the evening, hiring new bands and providing new types of music is a great way to stay new. As you introduce new types of music and bands, you will get a great sense of which musical groups bring the largest crowds. New bands allow you to market your restaurant in publications which are not restaurant-related. For instance, if you hire a Latin band, it is a good idea to place in ad in a Spanish language magazine. This sort of cross-marketing can expand your reach dramatically.

Many restaurants, especially casual ones, include a social night or two during the week. This helps to bring in business during the slower days and can be quite popular with younger foodies. For instance, you might consider offering a food trivia night at your restaurant, giving a gift certificate to the winner. Some restaurants dim the lights and show a movie during a casual night. Other restaurants choose to include a karaoke night. For this reason, you want to include promotions which help to keep the mood light, fresh and new.

To remain 'new', it is important to perform daily maintenance to your restaurant. A restaurant which is not cleaned daily or has obvious signs of wear and tear will not seem new, no matter how compelling the marketing strategy. In the first few months, this might include simple tasks like washing the floor and dusting the walls. As your restaurant ages, table might become off-centred and plates might be chipped. Take care of these issues quickly if you want to retain that new restaurant feel.

Section [9]

The Numbers of Restaurant Success

So far, we have discussed creating a business plan and monitoring the financials of your restaurant. Since you are entering the restaurant business to make money, there is little need to explain why having a firm grasp on your financials is so important. However, we have not discussed the details of calculating the important financial measure of your restaurant.

As you can imagine, there are a number of ways to calculate the major values of your business. For instance, you can calculate your food cost in terms of each dish, or you can study the kitchen invoices versus total revenue. It is important to choose a method of calculation which makes sense for your business model. Hopefully, the following methods will help you create the most compelling and useful way to display your food calculations.

Before we discuss the methods for determining labour and food cost, it is important to remember that the profit margin and labour costs of restaurants vary from concept to concept. As a general rule, fine dining restaurants will have a higher percentage of labour and food costs when compared to quick service and casual restaurants. The labour laws of countries can vary greatly, making the labour cost of restaurants vary greatly as well. Some countries prefer tipping as the source of a servers income, so the labour cost for this type of restaurant will be naturally lower than a restaurant in a country without tipping. For this reason, it is a good idea to study the profit ratios of restaurants in your local region.

With this said, restaurants tend to have a profit margin which falls within a certain range. If you can keep your labour and food cost low, you might be able to pull off a profit of 30%. However, if you use expensive ingredients and require a large labour force to serve your meals, your profit margin might be as low as 10%. Make sure to study your potential profit in great detail before opening your restaurant.

CALCULATING FOOD COST

Before you calculate the cost of food, it is important to keep a few points in mind. First, it is important to make sure you use the same dates for both revenue and invoices. If you end up using invoices for 35 days and the revenue statement for 30 days, your food cost will be dramatically inaccurate. To calculate food cost, you will need to have a great sense of current inventory. For this reason, you will need to record your inventory at the conclusion of every night.

To correctly calculate food cost, try the following method:

1. Determine Beginning Inventory (inventory from day before target dates)
2. Calculate the total cost of Purchases
3. Determine Ending Inventory (inventory from the last target date)
4. Determine Total Food Sales

Once you have this data correct, you can calculate your food cost thus:

$$\text{Food Cost} = \frac{(\text{Beginning Inventory} + \text{Purchases}) - \text{End Inventory}}{\text{Food Sales}}$$

For example, consider the following:

£

Beginning Inventory = 100,000
Purchases = 20,000
Ending Inventory = 105,000
Total Food Sales = 50,000

$$\text{Food Cost} = \frac{(£100{,}000 + £20{,}000) - £105{,}000}{£50{,}000}$$

$$\text{Food Cost} = \frac{£15{,}000}{£50{,}000}$$

Food Cost = 0.3 x 100%

Food Cost = 30%

If you calculate this value and have a low food cost, you are probably having a great day. On the other hand, if your food cost is higher than expected, you might be having a demanding day. Luckily, there are a few common culprits when it comes to a high food cost.

The first task to complete, if you calculate a very high food cost, is to check your numbers again. In particular, check the invoice dates you used to calculate your purchases. If you included an invoice outside your target dates, your food cost will be dramatically off the mark.

Secondly, it might be a good idea to recount your initial inventory. Perhaps you counted too many cans or too many steaks into your calculation. For this reason, have the kitchen complete another inventory audit. Besides miscounting cans, check how cans apply to your calculation. On an invoice, cans are typically listed in terms of one case. If you count 5 cans and apply this number to the invoice without paying attention, you might multiply the price of the case of cans by a multiple of five. As you can imagine, this can greatly influence your overall food cost.

Sometimes, a kitchen will send items back to the supplier if they are not up to standard or are the wrong item. However, your invoice will still reflect the cost of the returned item. Make sure to clearly mark which items have been returned, and adjust the cost of the invoice. Make sure this is reflecting in your billing statements as well. If you forget to negate this cost, your food cost will be higher than the actual food cost.

By following this method and tips, you are sure to create a food cost scenario which is an accurate reflection of your actual food cost.

CONTROLLING LABOUR COST

Besides food cost, the cost of labour will be one of your largest expenses. For this reason, it is important to get a great sense of your cost of labour. As we discussed before, you want to minimize labour on slow days and maximize labour on busy days. With this said, it is still important to control your labour costs in a more mathematical way.

To gain the most useful sense of your labour costs, try applying the following method:

1. Divide your employees into categories. Categories should reflect the pay grade (salary) for each employee type. For instance, the Maitre D. and Executive Chef will be the highest salaries, while the kitchen assistants and general cleaners will have the lowest salaries. All employees who receive the same pay or salary should be included in the same group.

2. Add the total number of work hours for each pay category. For example, if you have 5 employees who earn £10 an hour and work 30 hours each, the total number of hours worked will be 150 hours.

3. Multiply the hourly rate by the total number of hours. Using the example above, you can quickly determine that the total wage will be £1,500.

4. Determine the weekly rate for salaried employees. For instance, if you pay a manager £52,000 a year, the weekly salary would be £1,000.

5. Add the wages of each pay group together in terms of weekly rates. This will give you a sense of your total labour cost per week.

Hitting Your Expected Profit Margin

After three months, you might get lucky and hit your desired profit margin. With this said, you might be making a profit, but not at the level you anticipated before the opening. Finally, you might still be losing money. If this is the case, you need to review your entire operation.

To start, it is best to discuss businesses who hit their expected profit margins. As you can imagine, a restaurant which makes its desired profit margin within three months is a highly organized and successful business. The marketing plan was effective, the staff hires were correct and the correct menu was created. If this is the case, make sure to continue on with the successful techniques which have worked so far. With this said, all restaurants can make more money, even if it is a small addition to your margin. For instance, if you make your profit margin, perhaps you can find a source of ingredients which are less expensive. You might find you can reduce your labour cost by 5% or so, a great addition when it comes to the end of month and year financial review. Just because your business is doing well does not mean there are no areas which cannot be improved.

You might have opened your restaurant and are making a profit, but you might not be making the profit you originally expected or anticipated. If this is the case, it is a good idea to review a few aspects of your operation. Make sure your menu items are priced correctly. If you are missing your profit margin by a few percentage points, a simple increase in prices might help. Be aware, if you increase your prices to hit your intended profit margin, make sure this increase is not obvious or easily felt by your audience, you might end up losing customers in the long run.

Beyond the simple trick of increasing prices, it is a good idea to review your labour schedule. Many times, a restaurant will lose money because they hire too many staff to start the restaurant. This is especially true for restaurants which open for breakfast from the day they open the doors. These restaurants tend to take a while to attract an all-day crowd, which causes a decrease in profit. If this is the case, you might consider closing for breakfast or accept the losses until it become busier.

Another great area to study if you are not meeting your profit margin is to study sales in terms of front of house and back of house. For most restaurants, especially fine dining restaurants, you want to split sales between the kitchen and bar. In other words, 50% of sales should come from the kitchen and 50% of sales should come from the bar. If your kitchen sales are top heavy, you will not hit your desired profit margin. Remember, you will make a lot more money selling alcohol, so if you are not selling a lot of alcohol, there is no way for you to hit your expected profit margin.

While making a profit is nice and hitting your desired profit margin is really nice, the reality is that most restaurants will not make money for the first six months to one year of operation. This is the reason why it is important to have a fair amount of cash on hand as you open the doors. Many times, a restaurant will need six months in order to achieve a decent level of customers on a weekly basis. It takes time to bring locals in and convince them to constantly eat at your restaurant. You need to give the kitchen time to hit its rhythm, a task which requires you to allow some flexibility with the overall food cost. You need to ask yourself which front of house employees are truly necessary for each day and hour of operation. If you are not making a profit at first, do not fear, you are not alone.

Instead, if you are not making a profit, it is time to turn back to your business plan. Ask yourself which tasks have been accomplished and which expectations are being met. Isolate the expectations which are not being met and focus on these tasks. Are you not getting the foot traffic you expected? Take time to review the foot traffic in front of the restaurant, and try and find ways to increase your success. Is your labour cost out of control? Try and reduce the restaurant hours, especially when it becomes painfully clear you are losing money on certain days and meals. Be honest with your assessment and ask advice from people whose opinions you trust. A thorough review is the best way to get on track in terms of making your profit margin.

How to Price Your Menu Items

Now that you have settled into your restaurant, you will have gained a great sense of which dishes are popular and which dishes are not.. You can compare the profit margin of each dish to determine your long term menu success. It is important to maintain recipes which prove quite popular and profitable. You might want to dump menu items which are not profitable and do not sell. These items can be quite detrimental to your bottom line.

In terms of items which do not sell, the largest loss is to your profit margin. To prepare these dishes, you will have to order foods which are perishable, and as you know, all perishable foods have an expiration date. If the food sits in your kitchen and needs to be thrown out due to spoiling, this will dramatically impact your profit margin. Instead, lose dishes which are not popular and replace them with dishes which are popular. Not only will you save money on perishable foods, you can dramatically increase the number of customers who come to your restaurant.

Sometime, a dish will be popular and not profitable. If this is the case, the best solution is to increase the price of the dish. People will continue to order the dish as long as you do not increase the cost very much. For instance, if you need to change the price of a popular dish, it is never a good idea to increase the price by 10%. If you need to trim the cost of the recipe to make more money beyond a 10% increase, you might consider reducing the size of the portion. Additionally, you can change the most expensive ingredient in the recipe. For instance, if you are serving grass-fed beef, perhaps it is a good idea to solve your food cost problem by finding a cheaper variety of meat. Essentially, you want to serve the same dish without the customer realizing what occurred to make your dish more popular. This balance is a real art, but the above tips should help.

Beyond the food, you should review the prices you are charging at the bar. Perhaps a drink takes too long to make, which can increase your labour cost. If this is the case, make sure to find a solution to make the drink quicker. Sometimes, the ingredients you use in cocktails will be too expensive. If your bartender is ordering supplies which can be made in-house, make the change as soon as possible. Finally, you can discuss the prices of your goods with your wine and alcohol suppliers. These companies are often flexible with their prices, so make sure to ask for discounts and rebates if possible.

Another place where prices can get out of whack behind the bar deals with portioning. Learning to correctly portion the liquor will influence your bottom line tremendously. For instance, if your bartenders are pouring heavy with the booze, you will lose a lot of money in the long run. Make sure your bartenders are well aware of the correct way to portion liquor. This will help you correctly price your menu.

When pricing a menu after you open, the art is less in the actual pricing and more in the realm of finding backend solutions. Backend solutions include correctly portioning foods and beverages, finding cheaper ingredients, and so on. Changing the prices in front of a consumer can be tricky, especially when you are a young restaurant. For this reason, changing prices should be seen as a last resort to make your profit margin. By finding the correct balance when it comes to pricing your menu beyond the opening, success will be much easier to attain.

Section [10]
How to Build a Loyal Clientele

In order to become a successful restaurant, it is imperative to build a loyal clientele. By far the most effective way of building a loyal clientele is by serving a high quality, consistent product. If you serve a meal with a higher degree of quality, you are sure to stand out among your competition. In time, restaurant customers tend to migrate to restaurants which serve high quality fare, and you are sure to benefit from this behaviour.

Beyond quality, there are a number of additional tricks you can employ to build a loyal restaurant clientele. For one, giving your guests the VIP treatment each time they dine in your restaurant will help tremendously when it comes to building a loyal customer base. Loyalty cards, carrying free meals and other promotions will help to draw customer back. As always, social media is a powerful tool for building a constant message in the consumers mind.

Other techniques which are usually employed when building a loyal clientele include going off the menu. Giving your customers the first chance to taste a new menu item can be a powerful tool to make your loyal customers feel special. Finally, special promotions and events work well. Perhaps you might decide to close the restaurant for a night and treat your loyal customers to a closed VIP meal. While you might not make much money by closing your doors in one night, you are sure to bring greater profits in the long run.

This chapter was designed to help you understand some of the basic devices you can use to build a loyal clientele. It is very important to develop techniques which fit the needs and desires of your long term customers.

Since you have opened your restaurant for quite some time (months), remember to turn to your data when composing your long term relationship strategies.

Quality

By far, the most important strategy to build a long term loyal customer base is to serve a high quality meal. As mentioned before, you might serve nine wonderful meals to a particular client, only to serve a less than stellar meal on the tenth try. While you did a great job nine times in a row, the tenth attempt caused you to lose a loyal customer. Do this a couple hundred times, and you will quickly be out of business. For this reason, remember to maintain a high quality meal.

It is easy to say, "serve a high quality meal", but understanding what a high quality meal consists of is a different story. A few examples will help you comprehend the essence of a high quality meal.

For our first example we turn to the sandwich shop. Imagine a newly constructed restaurant with a very clean and concise menu, brand and atmosphere. You make great bread and serve artisan meats. Yet, your lettuce tends to wilt in the sandwich display. A customer comes to your restaurant and is served a sandwich with the sub-par lettuce. He notices the lettuce and vows to never return. He gets sick from the lettuce, vows to never come back, and tells his friends.

For the second example, we consider the fine dining restaurant. A loyal customer comes once a week for his favourite steak. The restaurant is beautiful and the service is great. While the quality of the meat is extraordinary, the new cook keeps overcooking the £100 steak. The loyal customer no longer shows up on Tuesday night.

With these two stories, I hope to convey the story of precision and an appreciation for details. While you might consider 99% of the quality issues of your restaurant, neglecting the 1% can have disastrous consequences. This is especially true over time. Losing one customer serves as a lesson. Losing dozens of clients tends to close the doors.

In order to maintain a quality meal, it is best to first start at the door. Every once in a while, make sure to discuss with the chef the performance of your suppliers. If a supplier is consistently giving you low quality foods, consider finding an alternative. From here, make sure the chef does not order too much on the inventory. Ordering too much will cause you to serve lower quality meals as well as increase your food cost. Finally, make sure you test the food all the time. Order a dish from the kitchen and make sure it is of the standard you have set forward with the kitchen.

Beyond quality food, you need to make sure you continue to serve a high quality meal. Not in terms of the food, but in terms of the service. The front of the house should always remain clean and organized, and the service staff should always remain attentive. Once you see waiters checking their mobile phones in the middle of a busy service, it is time to complete a quality assessment. Beyond the behaviour of the waiting staff, make sure the bar section of your restaurant continues to serve the same quality drinks. If you are going through a lot of bar staff, make sure the quality of the drinks has not shifted from the original creations to present. Remember, a complete commitment to quality will go a very long way.

Giving your Audience the VIP Treatment

I like to think there are two types of VIP treatment. The treatment you give to each and every guest (who should ALL be treated like VIPs), and the treatment you give to loyal customers. While it is important to treat all guests as VIPs, the people who bring you the most business deserve the most select and tailored service. For one, make sure to remember the names of your loyal guests, their favourite drinks and food. If your loyal customers come to your restaurant on an anniversary, for example, it's always a good idea to write this information down in a calendar. The next year they come to celebrate their favourite meal, being greeted for their special occasion will certainly make the night a bit more special.

In order to treat your VIPs to an enhanced experience, there are a few additional tricks to try. For one, consider buying your loyal guests a free drink before the meal. Popular in many independent restaurants in America, this tactic will keep your repeat customers happy each time they come to the restaurant. This is especially helpful in areas of the world where buying the guests' drinks is unpopular.

Some restaurants lure loyal clients to their tables by going off the menu. For instance, if a repeat customer asks you to prepare a dish off the menu, it is always a good idea to say yes to his or her request. Many times, customers who eat out on a nightly basis find a restaurant they like to eat in, but would prefer their own favourite dish. This sort of customer is typically willing to pay more for their dish. If you keep this type of customer happy, they tend to come two or three times a week. For this reason, always consider special orders for your more loyal customers.

A great way to build a loyal clientele is to have your staff memorize the names of your VIPs. For instance, every time a loyal guest comes to your restaurant with, let's say, business clients, addressing your client by his or her last name will be recognized by both your customer and his clients. A simple, "Hello Mr. Jones" can go a long way. For high frequency customers, make sure to hold tables or make room for them on very busy nights. While you will be ecstatic to serve a packed house, never forget those who are most loyal to you. If a customer comes with a group of people every Friday night, do your best to reserve the table.

As mentioned before, the best way to keep a loyal customer happy is to study the individual needs of each particular customer. For instance, one customer might shy away from alcohol, so you need to find a beverage solution which keeps them happy and is alcohol free. Another customer might prefer you make a dish with olive oil instead of butter. Make sure follow your VIP requests in order to maintain long term relationships.

Loyalty Cards

Loyalty cards can be a great way to bring customers back to your restaurant. This is especially true when it comes to quick service and casual restaurants. For example, if you own a quick service restaurant and serve 1,000 meals per day, there is very little chance you will be able to memorize the needs of each of your loyal guests. Instead, when you serve a large amount of meals, the best way to manage your loyal customers is through a Loyalty Card. Luckily, there are a number of ways to market and study loyalty cards.

Many quick service and fast casual restaurants keep their loyalty cards rather secret. Instead of advertising and handing a card to every customer, the staff retain the cards and give them to customers who they recognize as repeat customers. Secret loyalty cards make your loyal customers feel special, a task which is hard to manage when you serve thousands of meals a day. In terms of content, you might decide to award your loyal customers points in order to redeem free food or merchandise. Or, you might decide to take a more direct route. For instance, receive a free meal on every tenth purchase. Once again, make sure to study the needs and desires of your loyal customers before implementing loyalty cards.

Some food service establishments advertise their loyalty cards. For instance, the restaurant might charge £25 for a loyalty card, but offer a 5% discount on each and every purchase thereafter. While this might seem like an expensive proposition, gaining a loyal customer over time will make the 5% discount seem like a moot point.

Fine dining restaurants are not known for loyalty cards. Instead, a fine dining restaurant tends to rely on recognizing the individual guests. This starts when the guest calls the restaurant to make a reservation and extends to the behaviour of the staff. With this said, make sure to track the data of your loyal customers. Remember how often these clients come to your restaurant, what they order, how many guests they bring, and so on. Instead of collecting this data on a loyalty card, a formal restaurant keeps this data in a well-organized book. Some fine dining restaurants, however, do offer loyalty cards. Instead of providing cheap loyalty cards, the cards tend to be sleek in appearance and have a unique identifying number on the card. In many ways, these cards resemble credit cards. If you open a fine dining restaurant and plan on giving away loyalty cards, make sure the loyalty cards reflect the quality of the restaurant.

Beyond keeping your frequent customers happy, a loyalty card gives you a tremendous amount of data in terms of repeat customers. By analyzing the data of each card, you can determine which time your repeat customers come to your restaurant, on which day, which items are popular with loyal customers, how much they spend, and what complimentary items they order. For instance, if you own a sandwich shop and notice your loyal customers tend to order complimentary items such as iced tea, you might consider creating an iced tea recipe exclusively for your loyal customers. Once again, make sure to study your data then compose a loyalty card strategy which keeps your customers constantly happy.

SOCIAL MEDIA DISCOUNTS

A great way to build a loyal clientele is to build a robust social marketing campaign. As the weekend nears and people start to make their dining plans, adding a discount within the social media realm can draw people to your restaurant. The nature of social media is constantly changing. For this reason, the suggestions in this sub-section might not be relevant in two or three years. Remember, it is important to know what your loyal clients want, and this is especially true in regards to social media.

The two largest sources of loyal customers from social media can be currently found through Facebook and Twitter. Both platforms can serve your restaurant in a number of ways, so it is important to identify which techniques work well in your local area. To accomplish this, study your competition. Observe the Facebook and Twitter accounts of other restaurants in your area to discover how they draw in crowds. Do they offer specials? Do they post new and unique menu item descriptions or photos? Do they promote the local football club? Do they recognize their loyal customers by mentioning them in twitter feeds? These are just a few questions you should consider when studying the competition.

Once you have studied the competition, the next step is to put together your social media strategy to entice loyal customers. Beyond the message, you need to get a good sense of the most effective time and days to promote your restaurant. For instance, if you plan on offering a promotion on Saturday night, Monday night might not be the best time to post your offer.

It is often difficult to judge how popular your social media campaigns end up being. Not every guest who comes to your restaurant will take you to the side to confirm your social media campaign brought them to your restaurant. Instead, you need to monitor social media yourself. Do people add your location to their Facebook feeds when dining out? Are you mentioned in any tweets? Find the best strategy to discover this information. In time, you will compile a comprehensive and effective social media strategy in order to build a loyal customer base.

GOING OFF THE MENU

A great way to build a loyal clientele is to create menu items which are not listed on the menu. For instance, many quick service restaurants have found secret menus a great way to build a loyal and cult-like clientele. If you serve burgers, this process might include a special bacon variety or it might include an extra-large burger. If you are a fine dining restaurant, the off-the-menu dish might be a new concoction the chef is trying out. No matter what type of restaurant you decided to open, there are a number of benefits to the secret menu.

There are many ways to create a secret menu. Sometimes, a restaurants' secret menu will be tailored to each guest. For instance, if a guest constantly orders the same dish with the same modifications, you might consider naming the dish after the customer. The next time the customer arrives, you can tell the customer their dish is now part of the secret menu. Your loyal customer will be quite honoured with the listing, even if it is just known to a few people.

For other restaurants, the secret menu is better known. The 'secret' menu is advertised in local media and social media sights, but it is not given to each guest who enters the restaurant. Instead, the customer has to ask for the menu to unlock the key.

The content of a secret menu can vary greatly. However, make sure to use as many ingredients as you can from the normal menu. If you have a number of unique dishes on the secret menu but no one asks for the menu for a few days, you will be in trouble in terms of food cost. Instead, try and create a secret menu which makes use of one unique ingredient and your current ingredient list. Alternatively, try increasing the portion size when it comes to a secret menu item. Remember, secret menu items need to be unique and provide a sense of value which goes beyond the food on the plate.

Besides serving a secret menu, there are a number of ways to share off-the-menu items with your guests. If you are open for a holiday, try and serve the traditional foods of the holiday. For instance, if you are open on the day of the American Thanksgiving Holiday (last Thursday in November), try and serve a traditional Thanksgiving dinner. While it is hard to sell this meal on Thanksgiving in America (since everyone is eating at home), you might be surprised by the number of expats who come to your special meal. As always, promote the event through social media and other avenues when appropriate.

A common technique when it comes to serving meals which are not on the menu involves daily specials. Many people consider daily specials as part of the menu. However, since both the menu and the number of specials can change from day to day, a daily special menu should be an off-the-menu experience. Daily specials are a great way to sell foods which are reaching their expiration date. During the course of the business week, your suppliers will approach you with special deals. Paying close attention to these offerings, and creating specials based on these discounted foods can be a great way to fatten your bottom line.

There are many ways to reach your customers through off-the-menu items. By creating secret menus and daily specials, you will find it easy to attract two distinct types of customers. Your customers will have a unique topic to discuss with their friends, creating a viral momentum for you when it comes to building a loyal clientele.

SPECIAL EVENTS AND PROMOTIONS

Besides offering discounts through social media and loyalty cards, offering special events and promotions is a great way to build long term relationships in the restaurant business. There are many, many ways to promote your restaurant through special events and promotions. For this reason, it is important, as always, to determine the needs and desires of your clientele before implementing special events. Make sure to ask your loyal customers what sort of special events will be most attractive to them.

The first type of special event you might consider involves holidays. For instance, if you open a fine dining or casual restaurant, you might consider an exquisite New

Year's Celebration. Create a special menu for the night and include Champagne and drinks. Offer tables to your most loyal customers first, and offer a discount to your most loyal customers. Besides the New Year, there are a number of great days to hold special events. These days tend to vary from country to country, so it's important to find a list of holidays in your country. With this list, determine which days are best for special events. Begin to plan the event early and market early to bring in the most loyal customers on such special evenings.

Holidays are not the only days to promote a special event. For instance, many restaurants, especially casual ones, offer promotions on a weekly basis. For instance, restaurants with an appropriate setting do rather well when serving a Movie Night, a night with a meal themed around the movie being screened. Some restaurants find trivia to be a great way to bring new customers. If your restaurant is a sports bar, make sure to include trivia which is only sports related. For college and university towns, it is a good idea to have trivia content which is geared towards the college crowd. Music is another great theme to include for a trivia night. Prizes are important for this sort of event.

If you decide to throw a music trivia night, determine the prizes based on the size of the crowd. Let's say 200 people show up for the trivia night. If each person spends £30, the revenue for the night will be £6,000. You might consider prizes with a total budget of £600. Perhaps a free guitar to the winning team will help bring more people to the event next time. Gift certificates to your restaurant work great as well, but make sure to offer additional prizes outside the realm of your business.

There are other great themes to promote when holding a special event. If you live in a football centred town, it is always a great idea to hold a meal which promotes the team or a charity of the team. Casino nights are also a great idea for bar-centred restaurants. While local regulations might not allow you to keep the winnings of the night, you will most likely be allowed to give the profits to a charity of your choice. As with all keys to long term success, make sure to study the wants and desires of your audience.

As you grow your restaurant form year to year, you will learn which special events draw the largest crowds. Make sure to stick with these concepts and stay away from concepts which are less desirable to your audience. While special events can be quite helpful, they can also hurt your restaurant. This is especially true when your locals grow tired of undesirable events. If this is the case, you will quickly lose a significant and powerful client base. Instead, make sure to include special promotions in your restaurant, but at a level which is comfortable to your core audience; the people who come to your restaurant to eat a great meal.

Forging Long Term Relationships

As your restaurant grows from year to year, the most powerful customers you have will be the customer base which has remained loyal over the long run. These long term relationships are the key to your success. Failure to maintain long term relationships can cause your business to close in the long run. For instance, a town only consists of a set number of people. Even with tourists, you will need to rely on the local population for day-to-day survival. If you serve a bad meal to each person in your town once, you will soon have an empty dining room. For this reason, it is very important for you to build long term relationships.

There are many ways to define a long term relationship. Sometimes, a long term relationship involves your interaction with customers. Other times, a long term relationship involves a supplier or an employee. If business is slow for six months in your fourth year of business, these relationships are rather important. Let's say you are having a hard time with cash flow. If you cannot pay your supplier for a month or two, a long term supplier will be happy to help you through this difficult time. If you have changed suppliers many times in the first three years, you might not find the same level of understanding from your ever-changing suppliers. The same can be said for a long term employee. A long term employee is very much interested in the long term success of the restaurant. If they need to take a temporary pay cut to make it through thin times, they will be much more approachable if you have a great relationship. Just make sure to take care of them when you start making a profit once again.

Another relationship which is important in the long run involves the landlord. Many times, a restaurant will sign a three, five or ten year lease. When your lease expires and the landlord decides on a new rent, your relationship with the landlord will influence the price you pay. If you are considerate and treat the property with care, your landlord will most likely give you favourable terms for the next lease. Remember, the landlord wants to make sure the space remains successful and well cared for. Changing restaurant owners is a big risk, so the landlord will want to keep your successful restaurant. The relationship of landlord to tenant remains very important in the long run.

Within this chapter, we have spent a lot of time speaking about the ways in which you can build a loyal clientele over time. Over the years, you will get to know your most loyal customers. Just not on average nights, but during anniversaries, birthdays, graduations, and so on. For this reason, you will become a part of their lives, and they will become a part of the restaurants' story. Forging long terms relationships can mean many things to a restaurant, which is why it is important to find your own way of forging these relationships. Pay attention to the needs of your guests, but also consider your own ability and desire to interact with your guests. In time, you will learn to how to master this important relationship.

Section [11]

Keeping your Restaurant Model Modern Current and Relevant

When you first open a restaurant, your operation is considered modern and new. Over time, the new child which is your restaurant will become less relevant, at least when compared to your original business model. For this reason, it is very important to update your restaurant every year from the inception of your business. Luckily, there are many ways to keep your restaurant modern, current and relevant.

The changes you make to your restaurant can be small and minor to large and major. During the first few years of your operation, the changes you make should be small and minor. As the years pass (perhaps in terms of three, five and ten years) it is important to make major changes to your restaurant. By choosing a path of small and large changes over time, you are sure to keep your restaurant relevant.

Minor changes to your restaurant can include simple menu changes to a new coat of paint. You might decide to buy new plates for the restaurant or new glassware. Perhaps the uniforms of the staff should be updated, or you should update the style of music in your restaurant. Minor changes take a small amount of time to implement and can be accomplished on a small budget.

Major changes to your restaurant are a different beast. If you decided to add a new dining room to your property, this major change might require you to gain a new liquor license, building permits, tables, chairs, and so on. This major change will cost a lot of money and time. Beyond building a new wing to your restaurant operation, major changes might also include buying new tables and chairs, new kitchen equipment, moving the bar, changing the layout of your restaurant, to name a few. Major changes take time to implement, so make sure to spend months on the planning process before implementing these changes.

In this chapter, we discuss topics which will help you decide how and when to change. While you want to implement new changes to your restaurant, you need to make sure you adhere to the aspects of your concept which have proven successful and popular with your loyal customers. For this reason, it is important to discuss the most efficient and effective ways to study change in your restaurant.

UNDERSTANDING TRENDS

The easiest and cheapest way to determine the best way to keep your restaurant relevant is to understand the trends of the food industry. Besides trends which are relevant to your country and local region or city, it is important to understand trends from around the world. By studying the complete scope of global trends, you can determine which concepts will work well in your restaurant and which will not work so well.

While it is a nice idea to study global trends, you might have opened a restaurant with a regional theme such as French or Italian. Instead of focusing on global trends, you might want to focus on the trends within the mother country of your cuisine. For instance, if you open a French restaurant, make sure to travel to France from time to time to see which menu items and presentations are popular at the moment. Spend time on a few French food websites to determine what the media is talking about, what chefs are creating, and so on. Using these notes, you can compile menu changes, changes in service, changes in your bar menu, and so on. This is a great way to add minor changes to your restaurant.

Beyond regional cuisines, there are many other types of trends to pay attention to. Trends are especially important for quick service and casual restaurants, and these trends tend to be observed on a global level. For instance, a quick service restaurant style might be wildly popular within a short year throughout New York and Boston. By knowing this trend, you can implement the changes to your food concept in the United Kingdom. Since it takes two or three years for a food trend to cross the ocean, you will have plenty of time to implement this trend in your fast casual restaurant. Before you make major changes to your menu and signage, try sharing the new menu concept on your secret menu to judge potential success. Once again, the secret menu can help guide your future restaurant trends.

In terms of trends, there are two main categories you need to consider. Long term trends and short term trends. Short term trends are momentary bursts of enthusiasm in a particular recipe or style of cooking. These short term trends tend to be very popular in the summer months. Beyond the summer months, short term trends tend to be very popular with journalists who serve the general public. For instance, a newspaper will discuss a summer BBQ trend with great enthusiasm. While this trend might help you in the short term, the overall strength of the trend will be rather low. For this reason, you need to be able to identify short term trends.

Long term trends tend to be outlined in trade magazines. For this reason, make sure to read industry magazines often. Over time, make sure to observe which predicted trends become true and which remain false. If a particular magazine is rather bad at predicting trends, you are best to take this information with a pinch of salt. At the same time, you might find some magazines and trade journals provide a very accurate roadmap of the future. Pay attention to these trends as often as possible.

Beyond a global, media and national reach, you can find trends in your backyard. In particular, you should study the trends of your local competition. In other words, study your local competition and learn which restaurants are good at adapting trends. From here, learn what trends they have implemented then adapt this trend to your own restaurant. By studying your local trends, you will attract a larger local audience.

KNOWING WHEN AND WHAT TO CHANGE.

Knowing when to change and what to change is a critical part of your long term success. While you might think spending a lot of money to implement changes will pay off in the long run, this is not always the case. Instead, you need to create a more rhythmic style of change in your restaurant. Think of it as walking down a set of steps instead of jumping off a cliff. It is best to make small changes and measure your progress before making greater changes. Using this metaphor, it becomes easy to find the correct time to change as well as find the best way to change.

To start, we turn to the WHEN part of the equation. Luckily, it is rather easy to determine when you should change, or at least when you should consider changing. While you might put together a dynamic schedule to update your restaurant, when the time comes, you might find the change is not needed. For this reason, feel free to pass over specific change dates if you feel no work is truly needed.

The first moment you should consider change is at the three month mark after the opening. Judge the menu and observe which dishes are profitable and which are not. Update your menu to reflect these changes. Then, at the six month mark, you should review the same data and make changes as needed. In fact, the three month schedule in terms of menu changes is very popular, especially with seasonal restaurants. During this time, you might decide to make minor changes as well. Some minor changes include changing plates, silverware, menu designs.

As year one approaches, you might consider completing a more thorough study of your menu in order to implement changes. Beyond the menu, the one year-mark is a great time to have your restaurant professionally cleaned and painted. Completing a thorough cleaning every year will not only help to maintain your restaurant, but it will also instil a sense of cleanliness and sanitation. Restaurants which fail to clean from year to year quickly seem dirty and worn down. For this reason, make sure to clean your restaurant in great detail every year.

Your next update phase for implementing changes should be the three- to five-year mark. Here, you might consider buying new tables and chairs, new kitchen equipment, POS system, etc. You might also consider more major changes to the restaurant; changing the location of a bar, adding windows or moving the kitchen, for example. For this, the changes you make during the three- to five-year period should reflect necessary structural updates to your restaurant as well as aesthetic updates which are observed by your customers.

Finally, if you are a successful restaurateur for a long period of time, you might consider changes at the seven-, ten- and fifteen-year mark. By this time in your operation, you are most likely a local institution, so you want to maintain those aspects of your operation which remain popular. At the same time, you want to maintain aspects of your operation which give your restaurant character and charm. If your bar has significant wear from people standing at it for over ten years, the marks added to the bar might be rather pleasing to your customers, both new and old. For this reason, long term changes should reflect necessary structural improvements. A new dishwasher, oven, stove or flooring might be a few options to try.

While it is important to implement changes to your restaurant, it is important to know what and when to change. While the *when* part of the equation is easy to map out, the *what* part is a bit more difficult. Because of this, it is important to spend time understand what changes your loyal customers would like to see in your operation. By approaching changes with caution, suggestions and data, you will keep your restaurant modern and relevant for years to come.

NEW COMPETITORS

Now that you have been open for quite some time, you are likely to see new concepts open in your area, creating new competition for your restaurant. While you enjoyed your time as the new kid on the block, you now need to focus your attention on new competition. Luckily, there are a number of great techniques to implore in order to make sure new competition does not force you to shut your doors.

Make sure to visit your new competition when they open their doors. Remember, you will have a lot of experience when it comes to pricing and dining trends, so make sure to determine which factors your competitors are doing correctly and what factors they will most likely fail at. Study what trends they add to their menu, and determine how these trends compare to those in your own restaurant. If needed, implement a few changes to your menu in order to retain interest in your own restaurant. For instance, if a new concept creates a popular new salad, you might consider creating a similar dish for your customers. This will certainly help to keep loyal customers in your restaurant.

Beyond menu items, it's a good idea to study the marketing and advertising trends of your customers. If a competitor has a very big opening, you can probably learn a lot from their campaign. It has been years since you opened and your marketing plan might no longer be relevant. By studying your new competition, you can learn which new techniques are being employed to bring customers into the restaurant. Perhaps it is a social media trend or the signage of the new restaurant which works. Study these techniques and implement then into your own restaurant.

New competitors can be very dangerous when it comes to your own long term success. When a new restaurant opens, the chance of you losing a loyal customer increases dramatically. Sometimes, this change has nothing to do with the quality of the meal you serve or the ambiance of your dining room. Instead, sometimes you will lose a loyal customer because they are simply looking for something new. Make sure to reinforce your long term relationship with your clients when a new restaurant opens, and make sure to add elements of the new restaurant to your own business in order to retain your customers.

STAFF DEVELOPMENT

Over time, the front of house staff of a restaurant can become comfortable with their surroundings. Instead of being excited with every service, the staff will become a zombie-like crowd, simply performing tasks as needed. The engagement of the staff with the guests will become non-existent, a condition which can cause you to lose a significant amount of business, especially in the long run.

In order to keep your staff excited on a daily basis, it is best to put together a development plan. The goal of a development plan is to keep your staff happy with their positions as well as looking forward to events which mark their length of employment. For instance, if you have a staff member who has been loyal and hard working for five years, you might consider sending them on a vacation for a few days, compliments of the restaurant. This will not only keep your long term employee happy, it will breed a sense of long term benefits within the entire staff. Luckily, not all incentives need to be vacation related.

For instance, you might decide to offer a free meal for your staff member and a guest on a yearly basis. This tends to reduce the cost of the benefit, and helps the staff observe the entire restaurant process. It is particularly a good idea to allow the kitchen staff to eat in the dining room with this arrangement. Here, they can get a sense of the work the front of house staff does on a daily basis, and will help to instil a customer oriented approach to cooking in the kitchen.

Staff development might include trips to a local winery, supplier or farmer. Here, your staff will learn more about the foods they serve as well as the source of the foods. Beyond trips, staff development might include giving your employees great books about the industry. Here, the staff can read and learn about the style of food you serve, the financial of a restaurant and why they are important, social behaviour of customers, to name a few topics.

Staff development is all about finding a way to keep each member of your crew happy with their personal growth within the organization. For this reason, it is important to consider the type of staff you hire and the type of restaurant you open when putting together a development schedule. Make your staff feel like they are an important part of the operation and that you are concerned with their long term development in the industry. In time, you are sure to create a staff base which is current and relevant.

TIME TO EXPAND SERVICES, DEVELOP ADDITIONAL SEGMENTS

Now that you have settled into your restaurant, it is time to consider ways of increasing business. Sometimes, this can be achieved by adding to the hours of operation of your restaurant. Other times, it might include expanding your physical space. Finally, you might consider finding additional segments to develop. This can be achieved through catering.

The easiest way to expand your services is to increase the hours of your operation. For instance, you might be open for six days a week. By opening on the seventh day of the week, you can easily increase your business. Beyond opening on new days, you can extend your hours into the early morning or late night. If this is the case, put together a well-organized breakfast menu as well as a well-organized late night menu. These two techniques can help you remain relevant.

Beyond opening for more hours, you might be able to expand the size of your restaurant. Many restaurants in cities do not have this option, so it might be hard to implement. This problem is compiled if you have a landlord. Instead, you might be able to move your kitchen to a second floor, basement or back of the restaurant. Sometimes, if you create a more efficient kitchen you can reduce the size of the kitchen. If this is the case, you might consider expanding the size of your dining room. An extended dining room can give your restaurant new life, keeping it modern and relevant.

The final way to open a new segment in your restaurant is to open a catering service. Now that you have built a loyal customer base and become quite comfortable with the size of your operation, you can start to take on more complicated menus for customers which are served outside the restaurant. Sometimes, a catering event will include preparing and delivering food. Other times, your operation might include a more formal service off-site. Either way, catering sales can dramatically increase the amount of business you perform on a weekly basis. Besides the increase in business, catering is a great way to expose your business to new customer bases. For this reason, make sure to market your catering events as often as possible.

Expanding your services can be a dramatic event, so it is very important that you proceed with caution. For instance, if you open for breakfast but end up not attracting a lot of business, you will end up losing a lot of money in terms of labour cost. The same can be said for a catering operation. Perhaps you hire an additional five waiters to handle to added catering load. If your catering business does not take off, you are sure to lose a lot of money. For this reason, take great care when expanding your service.

THE FUTURE OF THE SOCIAL MEDIA RESTAURANT

Social media will probably remain the most effective tool you have to build a long term restaurant which retains its modern feel. For this reason, it is important to constantly pay attention to marketing and advertising trends in terms of social integration.

It is very difficult to determine what the future of social media will look like in five or ten years. It is even more difficult to give advice on what you should pay attention to. What seems like a rule of thumb today might not be so relevant in six months. For this reason, the best way to make sure your restaurant remains relevant and modern within the realm of social media is by studying trends.

To study social media trends, it is a good idea to follow a few blogs which deal with social media integration. By paying attention to the thoughts of social media experts, you can gain a significant edge over your competition. Social media blogs tend to be a few months ahead of the trends felt by consumers, so paying attention to their thoughts and feelings can be helpful to you. Among future social media trends, paying attention to experts is a trend which will not grow old.

LISTENING TO FEEDBACK AND REVIEWS

As you settle into your restaurant, the most important source of information in regards to your operations will be your customers. Customers will give you feedback directly or through comment cards. Make sure to thank your customers for their support as well as suggestions, and implement changes as needed. Remember, your best source of feedback is found through an honest conversation with your customers.

Reviews are a great way to judge the success of your restaurant. With this said, the internet has allowed everyone to be a food critic. You are likely to discover negative reviews on *Yelp* and other review sites. The goal is to have overwhelmingly positive reviews on such sites. You will never get 100% positive reviews, but you should shoot for 95% positive reviews. Consumers can sift through negative news to a point. If 50% of your reviews are negative, it will be hard for a customer to accept the fact that the reviews might be wrong.

Beyond internet reviews, the local media in your area will spend time reviewing your restaurant. Make sure to pay attention to their reviews, and when the reviews are very good, add this to your marketing materials. You want to make sure you highlight your good reviews. For instance, you might consider framing your good reviews and displaying them on the outside of your restaurant. As people walk by and read the review, they are more likely to try your restaurant in the future or during that particular day.

Reviews and feedback are an important part of running a successful restaurant. Reviews and feedback give you great guidance in terms of your current and future menu offerings, helpfulness of the staff as well as look and feel of the restaurant. While you will occasionally have a bad review, you will also receive a lot of positive and helpful reviews. Make sure to learn from them all.

When it comes to bad reviews, you need to make the wrong become a right. By acknowledging the mistake, and fixing it to the best of your ability, you will get a positive review from the person who gave you the bad review. You need to make it known you are acknowledging reviews and feedback, but also that you are appreciating it and would welcome more of it. You may want to reward the 'best review or feedback' of the month. Reviews are a great avenue of social media growth for the restaurant business.

ASSOCIATIONS AND INDUSTRY COLLABORATIONS

Beyond learning from your customers, another key to running a restaurant, which is modern and relevant, involves local associations and collaborations. For instance, a great way to keep the walls of your restaurant modern and relevant is to feature a local artist for six months or so. Not only will your customers have a chance to support a local artist, your restaurant might be featured in an art centred magazine. This type of cross marketing can serve all parties involved.

Sometimes, it is a good idea to contact your local chamber of commerce and restaurant association to inquire about membership. Study the benefits of each association, and join the groups which can help your business the most. Many local chambers' of commerce promote their local businesses throughout the area. Joining this type of group can bring credibility to your restaurant, as well as introduce you to the businesses in your area.

Trade associations are a great resource for restaurants as well. For instance, joining the local restaurant association will give you access to the full range of suppliers, but it will also provide you with access to experts in your local area. For example, you might find a company which specializes in helping restaurants market to the local audience, or you might find a contractor who specializes in restaurant construction. For this reason, consider joining a professional restaurant association.

Section [12]
Tips to Long Term Success

At this point in the book, you are well aware of the tasks required to open a restaurant as well as the tactics you need to employto keep your restaurant relevant. With this said, there are a few techniques and concepts you might want to keep in mind over the long run. These techniques can help you build a successful brand in the long run.

Some issues you might want to consider when it comes to long terms success include expanding the business. Opening a second location is a great measure of success and will increase your bottom line significantly. As we discussed, making minor and major changes to your restaurant are important, and with major changes comes a time when you might need to close the restaurant for a few days. In order to get through this process successfully, the following chapter will help.

Besides expanding and renovating, you might decide to change your concept to assure long term success. This chapter discuss some scenarios where concept change is acceptable. Finally, you may not remain successful after, let's say, five years. At this point, you might want to consider an exit strategy for your particular restaurant. To help you with this transition a few notes have been added for your benefit. Whether positive or negative, it is time to review your long term goals.

TIME TO EXPAND?

For restaurants that have remained very successful over the course of the first or second year of business, thoughts of expansion might be the next step of the business plan. This is especially true for restaurants of the quick service or casual variety. However, many fine dining restaurant empires can expand, but these restaurants tend to open new restaurants with a different themes. No matter what type of expansion you choose, the very fact that you are expanding is a great sign of a healthy business.

To start the story of expansion, we start with the quick service concept. Here, the layout, menu and ways of working will be clearly defined and easy to implement in another city. The best way to expand your quick service empire is by franchising your business model. Franchising brings investors to your business, which in turn pay you to open your concept in another market. In addition to an initial fee, you are likely to collect fees based on total revenue. In a sense, you need to do little work to make money when franchising. Instead, most of your work has been completed during your first opening. You have a proven business plan and a detailed employee manual. You have devised strategies in terms of how to prepare the foods and market the concept to the public. In order to franchise your business, you need organize this data into a clear and concise document. Ideally, the franchisee will be able to pick up your organized material and easily open the concept in less than six months. While you need to pay attention to the actions and performance of your franchisee, the amount of work per profit will make you rather happy in the long run.

Besides quick service restaurants, fine dining restaurants are known to expand from time to time. Instead of opening the same restaurant in a different city, a fine dining restaurant will instead open a different concept, but rely on the same systems of operation. For instance, the name and menu of the restaurant might be different, but the expanded restaurant will use the same suppliers, Point of Sales system, and employee manual, to name a few congruent tasks. When a fine dining restaurant opens another location, the business goes from being an independent restaurant to a restaurant group. This can be an exciting time for any restaurant!

Closed for Renovations

Now that you have been open for quite some time and have decided to undergo major renovations, the best place to start is to put together a plan. You will need to clearly determine what elements of the restaurant you want to change. If you are not clear with the changes you want to make, you can expect delays during the construction process. If you plan on closing for one week and end up being closed for one month, you are sure to suffer in the long run.

Instead, when you decided to close for renovations, you need to make sure you have all your tasks well studied and organized. Make sure you have discussed your time constraints with the contractor. Ask your contractor to order ALL supplies before the construction process begins. This will help to reduce delays. It is a good idea to add a clause to the contract just in case the contractor cannot complete the work within the allotted time period. Within the contract, make sure to include penalties if the contractor does not finish their work on time.

Besides the construction, there are many tasks for you to complete. Some of the tasks might include buying new glassware, plates and silverware. Other tasks might include buying new tables and chairs. No matter what the task, small or large, it is important to receive all of your remodelling supplies before you start the remodelling process. Items for your remodel might not arrive on time, and if you have a short rehab time frame, a delay in receiving your new wares will push back your re-opening date. To remove this possibility, make sure to receive all your supplies, no matter how small, before starting the construction. During this time frame, you might consider renting a storage unit to hold the new goods until needed. This way, there is no chance of the materials being adulterated by the restaurant staff, either on purpose or by accident.

Another important part of closing to remodel includes the day you should let your clients know you are closing to remodel. Besides letting them know the remodelling dates, it is important to inform of the new opening date. Here, you can gently persuade your loyal customers to come as soon as the re-opening arrives. To make sure your customers have plenty of time to adjust their schedules for your planned closing, it's a good idea to inform your customers one month before the remodelling date.

Beyond remodelling the front of the house, it is a good idea to spend time remodelling the kitchen. It might be a good idea to update the tiles and paint the kitchen. You might decide to remove the equipment and have it professionally cleaned to remove all traces of dirt and grease. The dishwasher might need changing, and the water lines should be cleaned. Updating the kitchen will help make your back of house seem refreshing, both to the kitchen staff and your customers. Yes, a clean kitchen tends to demonstrate itself to your customers.

Once you have finished the remodelling process, it is a good idea to share your remodelling with the world. Think of this remodel as the introduction of your 'version two' of the restaurant. In many ways, after you open again, you should brand your remodelled restaurant as a grand opening. Since you have spent money and time updating the space, make sure to share this change with the world. The press and public are sure to create a buzz for your updated ambiance.

When to Change Models

Sometimes, a restaurant will open and remain unsuccessful. While 90% of the menu is failing, you might find that 10% of the menu does very, very well. While these menu items are not special, they sell well and make a great profit. Once you study the numbers, you realize that by only selling the successful aspects of your restaurant, you will make a profit. If this is the case, you might consider changing your business model.

This scenario is not very likely in a fine dining restaurant, but it is very likely in a quick service or casual restaurant. A great example includes the complex menu of the quick service restaurant. For instance, when you open a quick service restaurant, you might be tempted to create a large and complex menu. In time, you realise that you only sell 10% of the menu. Perhaps pizza. You are losing a lot of money in terms of food cost. The best way to approach this problem is to simplify your menu and only sell what sells. If pizza sells and hamburgers do not, a simple twist to your concept might serve you rather well.

Many times, you might open a concept only to have a competitor open next door. A great example is opening a coffee shop and having a Starbucks open directly across the street. While you did well before the Starbucks came, your coffee business is beginning to lose money. To overcome this, you might consider rebranding your restaurant as a tea shop or coffee shop and pastry store. By offering premium products, you can easily overcome the burden of a big name brand. In addition, you might consider changing your concept to reflect a locally owned mentality. Buy the ingredients local, and emphasize that 100% of your business remains in the community. In this instance, a small change in your concept message can go a long way.

Sometimes, you might want to completely change your concept. Perhaps you opened an upscale restaurant and bar in a popular part of town. While the bar is doing exceptionally well, you might not sell a lot of food. While you do not sell a lot of food, you still need to pay for a kitchen staff and lost food due to spoiling. Instead of closing this sort of unprofitable business, you might consider closing the food section of the restaurant and open a full bar. Meaning, change the dining room into a second bar and sitting area. Sometimes in the restaurant business, your final concept finds you instead of you finding the concept. If this is the case, it is best to go with the flow of the locality. Besides, bars can make a great profit margin when managed correctly.

Deciding to change your restaurant concept can be a difficult pill to swallow. In many ways, it might seem like your business has failed. However, you need to keep in mind that the greatest measure of success in the restaurant business is making a profit. If you have a great concept but are not making a profit, but can develop a plan to make a profit, you are still considered a success in the restaurant business.

ALL CHANGE, EXIT STRATEGY

Sometimes in the restaurant business, the burden of losing money on a daily basis becomes too much. If this is the case, after sustained months and quarters of loss, you might consider closing the doors and moving onto the next restaurant concept you have in mind. While it might be difficult to accept the failure of your restaurant, it is important to remember the success you achieved during your time in business. Learn from the elements of your business plan which went wrong, and make sure to look out for these mistakes the next time you open a food business. Another consideration includes the fact that one market segment worked and you want to close the restaurant operation to concentrate on that particular segment. It can be anything from outside catering contracts to training catering staff to publishing in the industry. Just make sure to stick to your business strengths.

There are many tasks to complete if you choose to close your restaurant. Firstly, you need to inform the staff of the closing as well as the last day of business. You need to reassure the staff that they will receive great recommendations for future employees, and if you can, try to help them find new jobs. You need to cancel your food service permit as well as your liquor license. You need to pay your final sales tax and you need to settle with your suppliers.

When closing a restaurant, you can still make some money. Try and sell your glassware, plates, tables and chairs. The kitchen equipment, depending on the quality of the stove, oven, etc, can actually command a pretty penny. The same can be said for the bar equipment. Make a final inventory of your equipment and supplies, and try to recover 20% of the original cost of the equipment. While you might not make a fortune during the closing, at least you will make something.

If you are leasing a restaurant and decide to close, you can exit the space rather easily. On the other hand, you might own the property, which can actually be a blessing in disguise. Since you have created a restaurant and kitchen, your space is likely to quickly find a tenant. If this is the case, you can depend on income from another restaurateur, a much more stress-free aspect of restaurant ownership.

ALL SAID (WRITE A BOOK)

Throughout the course of this book, you have learned the ins and outs of running a restaurant. You will have learned how to correctly formulate a food concept, how to write a compelling business plan, how to navigate a restaurant opening and the keys to long term success. During this process, it is a good idea to write down your personal experiences with a restaurant opening. Using this guide and your notes, you might be compelled to write your own book on the opening process. Perhaps a book on the people you meet, learning the craft of running a restaurant, dealing with suppliers - these are just some of the issues you might discuss in your own restaurant book. Perhaps you might discuss the ethnicity or specialty type of restaurant you opened. Using this guide, experiences you draw from other aspects of your life, personal experiences, the good, the bad, the ugly; anything unique to you. Remember, your story might serve as the inspiration or identify for someone who aspires to be as successful as you are someday.

While you are sure to learn a lot by the contents of this book, as you can imagine, you are sure to encounter many events during your opening which are completely unexpected. Using the guidance mentioned in this book, you will hopefully find these unexpected events easy to deal with. Perhaps the greatest tool you can bring to the table is being extremely well organized. With this quality, you can quickly adapt to the needs of your business. Stay organized and the restaurant business will be a lot less stressful.

Finally, congratulations on deciding to open, or for even thinking about opening a restaurant, and thank you for taking the time to read this book. Hopefully, you have learned the ins and outs of running a business and have brought some clarity to the type of restaurant you want to open. During the opening process, it is a good idea to return to this book in order to make sure you are not forgetting important tasks before, during and after the opening.

Remember, within this book, there are many aspects that remain a guide or catalyst to your own imaginations and creativity. There are also a number of aspects which refer to the more practical aspects of opening a restaurant. Examples include training, consultancy and workbook. However, it is important to remember there are many external sources which might help you as well. Some consider training, scheduling, while others might include mediation, accounting, how to market, etc. I would highly recommend you to look out for and read these sort of resources. If you find these books or resources stimulating, they will be even more useful and productive when it comes to your actual success.

Finally, have fun with the opening and welcome to the adventure of being a restaurateur!

About The Author

Charles Okwalinga entered the restaurant business along with his supportive wife, Margaret, when they opened their first restaurant, Exceline, in London UK in 2003. Margaret, trained in Catering and Hotel Management and a very creative recipe formulator, partnered with Charles in founding their restaurant, a fine dining African Restaurant concept.

Being passionate in business development and customer services, Charles learned his experience, passion and diligence in running the restaurant that has stood in consistency and quality for 10 years, a success uncommon in the industry.

In running Exceline, Charles now has taken the knowledge, skills and experience in the industry and written this book and additional available materials, to assist those that are in it or thinking of joining and would need to focus of what it takes to be a successful restaurateur or establishment.

Charles was recognized and chosen as a leader in his role in the provision of African cuisine, to undertake Business Leadership training under the London Development

Agency Business leadership training programme in 2008, some of the insights he shares in this book.

Supported Charities Projects

Charles supports *'Business Fights Poverty'* as the world's largest community of professional harnessing business for social impact.

Charles believes that creativity and enterprise, forging productivity, is the best chance of victory in the fight against poverty.

Printed in Great Britain
by Amazon.co.uk, Ltd.,
Marston Gate.